THE METAPHYSICAL
ELEMENTS OF JUSTICE

The Library of Liberal Arts

OSKAR PIEST, FOUNDER

THE METAPHYSICAL
ELEMENTS
OF JUSTICE

Part I of The Metaphysics of Morals

Immanuel Kant

Translated, with an Introduction, by
John Ladd
Professor of Philosophy, Brown University

The Library of Liberal Arts
published by
The Bobbs-Merrill Company, Inc.
A Subsidiary of Howard W. Sams & Co., Inc.
Publishers • Indianapolis • New York • Kansas City

Immanuel Kant: 1724-1804

The Metaphysical Elements of Justice was
originally published in 1797

COPYRIGHT ©, 1965
THE BOBBS-MERRILL COMPANY, INC.
Printed in the United States of America
Library of Congress Catalog Card Number: 65–26538
First Printing

CONTENTS

THE METAPHYSICS OF MORALS

Part I
THE METAPHYSICAL
ELEMENTS OF JUSTICE

73333

The General Theory of Justice

I. PRIVATE LAW

Of Proprietary Rights in General in External Things

APPENDIX

Supplementary Explanations of the
Metaphysical Elements of Justice

INTRODUCTION

I. The Spirit of Kant's Moral and Political Philosophy

The key to Kant's moral and political philosophy is his conception of the dignity of the individual. This dignity gives man an intrinsic worth, a value *sui generis* that is "above all price and admits of no equivalent." [1] It is the source of his innate right to freedom, and from the right to freedom follow all his other rights, specifically his legal and political rights. Inasmuch as every individual possesses this dignity and right, all men are equal. Thus, Kant may be regarded as the philosophical defender par excellence of the rights of man, of his equality, and of a republican form of government.

In emphasizing the rights of the individual, Kant sets himself against every form of utilitarianism. He believes that neither morality nor law can be founded on social utility, the general happiness, or the common good; they are founded, rather, on the rights of individual man. Insofar as any course of action, private or public, conflicts with these rights, it is *ipso facto* wrong; and it is wrong regardless of the amount of good that may result from it. In this sense, he categorically repudiates the principle that the end justifies the means, however good and worthwhile the end may be. Thus, for example, he severely castigates those who hold that the aim of bringing Christianity and civilization to primitive societies justifies the use of violence and fraud against them. "The good of mankind" cannot be used as an excuse for such injustice. A theme throughout his political writings is the condemnation of the use of violence and fraud, and this explains his strictures against war and revolution.

[1] Kant, *Foundations of the Metaphysics of Morals*, trans. Lewis W. Beck, "Library of Liberal Arts," No. 113 (New York: Liberal Arts Press, 1959), p. 53.

From the conception of the dignity of man, summed up in the concept of freedom, Kant derives all his civil and political liberties. This conception not only demands the repudiation of slavery and all other forms of inequality, but also requires us to strive for a constitutional and republican form of government and, on the international level, for the abolition of war and the establishment of an international organization of states. These political objectives are obligatory, not because they are advantageous or useful for mankind, but because every individual has an inalienable right to be his own master and to live in freedom and peace. Freedom and peace are not "philanthropic ideals," but demands of justice.

We now have to ask: How does man come to possess this inherent dignity? What is the source of his rights and of his claim to freedom? Kant's answer is that they arise from the fact that each member of mankind is a moral being. In order to explain this, some reference must be made to the doctrine of the categorical imperative.

The classic statement of Kant's moral philosophy is contained in the categorical imperative, which says: "Act only according to that maxim by which you can at the same time will that it should become a universal law." [2] Practically, Kant argues, this amounts to the principle: "Act so that you treat humanity, whether in your own person or in that of another, always as an end and never as a means only." [3] Underlying the categorical imperative is the idea that every man gives the moral law to himself; that is, each individual is not only a subject, but also a sovereign legislator in the "realm of ends," the moral realm. The very conception of morality involves the notion of moral autonomy.

The condition that makes morality both possible and necessary is that man is a rational being possessing freedom, for freedom alone explains moral autonomy. "Freedom must be presupposed as the property of the will of all rational beings." [4]

2 *Ibid.*, p. 39.
3 *Ibid.*, p. 47.
4 *Ibid.*, p. 66.

There are two aspects of this freedom. Kant calls them "negative" and "positive freedom." *Negative freedom* is the capacity to act independently of foreign, external causes; in other words, it is freedom from external constraint. *Positive freedom*, on the other hand, is the "property of the Will to be a law to itself"; [5] that is, it is the property of autonomy. On Kant's view, the Will itself is the source of moral laws, as a self-legislator. It is this fact of positive freedom, that man subjects himself voluntarily to the moral law by legislating it for himself, that makes him a moral being and gives him dignity. (It should be noted that Kant does not want to say that man actually always acts morally, but only that each one of us acknowledges himself to be bound by moral principles.)

Negative freedom is a necessary condition of positive freedom, because a person must be negatively free in order to be positively free. In other words, a man can set the moral law to himself only if he is free from external constraint. Politics and law are concerned only with man's negative freedom, which it is their business to secure. (I shall call this negative freedom "liberty.") It is no business of the state or, for that matter, of other individuals to try to make men moral; only the individual can do that for himself. (Otherwise, he would not be autonomous; to make others moral is, for Kant, a self-contradiction.) Nevertheless, morality demands that man be negatively free, and in this sense, therefore, the demand for liberty is a moral one. Man's innate right to liberty has its basis in the negative freedom that is demanded as a condition of moral autonomy, that is, of morality itself.

Two general comments about Kant as a philosopher may be added here. First, he did not believe that it is the business of the philosopher to discover new principles of conduct, for he thought that every man knows in his heart what is right and what is wrong. (Politicians are, however, usually blinded by their greed for power; they need to be "reminded" that they, as much as others, are subject to the moral law.) Thus, we should not expect Kant to offer us a full-blown political or legal theory, with all the answers, so

[5] *Ibid.*, p. 65.

to speak. His purpose is, rather, to lay bare the principles underlying government and law and to provide a philosophical foundation for them. His aim is therefore much more modest than that of, say, Plato or Mill.

Second, despite the common conception of Kant as a system-builder, a close study of his writings will reveal that he is much more a discoverer of problems than a purveyor of answers. Every page of the present work can be read as a philosophical meditation on some problem concerning the relation of morality to politics and law. The treatise as a whole focuses on the fundamental problem of political philosophy, namely, the justification and limits of the use of coercion (or, in modern terms, the morality of power). Philosophically, this problem in its many ramifications leads inevitably to the question of the relation of the ideal (Idea) to the actual in politics and law. These are the themes that run throughout the *Rechtslehre*.

II. Divisions of Moral Philosophy

The title of the present work, *The Metaphysical Elements of Justice*, Part I of *The Metaphysics of Morals*, indicates its place in Kant's conception of moral philosophy.

"Metaphysics" is a technical term in Kant's philosophy. It stands for "the science which exhibits in systematic connection the whole body (true as well as illusory) of philosophical knowledge arising out of pure reason"; [6] that is, it is the body of synthetic a priori basic principles of a particular discipline. Insofar as these principles are concerned with how things do happen, that is, the theoretical knowledge of things (what we call "science"), it is called the metaphysics of nature; and, insofar as it is concerned with principles of what ought to happen, that is, practical knowledge leading to action, it is called the metaphysics of morals.

It is important to note that, for Kant, metaphysics as such

[6] *Immanuel Kant's Critique of Pure Reason*, trans. Norman Kemp Smith (London: Macmillan and Co., 1929), A 841=B 869.

is entirely a priori. Thus, the metaphysics of morals embraces only the pure a priori part of morals, in abstraction from its empirical component, and it must not be taken to constitute the whole of moral philosophy. Nevertheless, because the subject matter of the two parts of *The Metaphysics of Morals*, justice and virtue, involve the application of these a priori concepts to practice, the empirical part cannot be entirely neglected. Hence a completely pure metaphysics of justice and virtue is impossible, and so, instead of referring to their principles as "metaphysical basic principles" (*Grundsätze*), he prefers to call them simply "elementary principles" (*Anfangsgründe*).[7]

The metaphysics of morals, considered as pure moral philosophy (*Sittenlehre*), is divided into two parts: jurisprudence (*Rechtslehre*) and ethics (*Tugendlehre*), and these are concerned with justice (Law) and virtue, respectively.[8]

Kant draws the distinction between these parts in two ways that do not entirely overlap. His first distinction is between types of legislation, which he calls "juridical" and "ethical," respectively; the second distinction is between kinds of duties —those of justice and those of virtue.

Essentially, the distinction between juridical and ethical legislation relates to the kind of incentives involved in law as opposed to ethics. Kant holds that there are two distinct ways of being bound to do one's duty (*die Art der Verpflichtung*), namely, from the outside or from within. I may be obliged to do my duty by someone else, for example, by a political authority employing coercion or threats of coercion. This is what Kant calls "external" or "juridical" legislation; it entails the use of external coercion and involves the corresponding incentives to move me to do what is re-

7 See Preface, pp. 3–4.

8 Note that Kant uses the German *Sittenlehre* as a translation of the Latin *philosophia moralis* and *Rechtslehre* and *Tugendlehre* as translations of *jus* (or *jurisprudentia*) and *ethica*, respectively. Actually, he uses *Ethik* and *Tugendlehre* interchangeably. For an explanation of the meaning of *Recht* and *Rechtslehre*, see the next section.

quired. On the other hand, I may do my duty simply because it is a duty, in which case the Idea of duty is my only incentive, and I am coercing myself rather than being coerced from the outside. Kant calls this "internal" or "ethical" legislation.

Now, according to Kant, some duties may be required by both types of legislation simultaneously. For example, keeping a promise may be an object of both juridical and ethical legislation. If I perform such a duty simply because it is my duty, then my act may be said to be "moral"; if, however, I do it only because of some external coercion, then my act will be merely "legal."

We can now understand what Kant means when he defines justice (or Law) as the body of laws that are susceptible of being given in external legislation; for he thinks it of the essence of law that it prescribes duties that can be, although they need not be, externally enforced. In other words, law is a coercive order. All our duties as such, however, are prescribed by ethical legislation, even though some of them may also be prescribed by juridical legislation. In this sense, then, ethics may be said to encompass jurisprudence (or Law.)

The second distinction is between duties of justice and duties of virtue. Here Kant uses a fourfold classification of duties. The four types are: (1) perfect duties to oneself; (2) imperfect duties to oneself; (3) perfect duties to others; and (4) imperfect duties to others. A perfect duty ("narrow duty") is one the nonperformance of which is wrong; it is a duty owed. Keeping a promise would be an example of such a duty. An imperfect duty ("wide duty"), on the other hand, is one whose performance is meritorious, but whose omission is not an offense. Benevolence is an imperfect duty. Jurisprudence, that is, justice and Law, is concerned only with perfect duties to others (that is, #3). Kant calls these duties of justice.

Why justice (and Law) should be limited to this third class of duties should be immediately apparent if we remember that justice relates only to what is subject to external legislation. Only duties to others and those that are owed could satisfy this requirement of enforceability, for one obviously could not enforce duties to oneself and should not enforce duties the omission of which is not wrong. It follows from this that all duties that are not duties of justice are duties of virtue, and duties of justice and duties of virtue form two mutually exclusive classes of duties.

In sum, jurisprudence (Law) is distinguished from ethics in that (1) it is the subject of external legislation and (2) it relates only to duties of justice. Insofar as ethics is especially concerned with the duties of virtue, it excludes jurisprudence; but insofar as, in ethical legislation, it is generally concerned with all duties whatsoever, it also includes jurisprudence.

III. Law and Justice

It is impossible to understand the present work without taking into account the various meanings of the German word *Recht* and the special meanings assigned to it by Kant. To begin with, in German, as in other Continental languages, there are two words that can properly be translated by the English word, "law," namely, *Recht* and *Gesetz*. (In Latin, the equivalent words are *jus* and *lex;* in French, *droit* and *loi*.) Basically, the difference between these two terms is this: *das Recht (jus, droit)* is used for the corpus of laws and legal principles of a particular legal system; that is, it is what we call *"the* law." As such, it is a collective concept and has no plural form. It is here translated as "Law" (capitalized). *Gesetz,* on the other hand, is the word used for a particular law or statute, and it has a plural, "laws." It is here translated as "law" (uncapitalized). Etymologically, the word *Gesetz* is related to the verb *setzen*—to set, to posit, to lay down—so that *Gesetz* implies that it is something set or laid down by someone, for example, a legislator. Kant would very likely say that every law (*Gesetz*) implies a lawgiver or legislator; indeed, he conceives of the moral law itself as a kind of law that one gives—that is, legislates—to oneself. (This is his doctrine of autonomy.)

The expression *Recht* (*jus, droit*) also contains, however, an ambiguity that is not reflected in English, for, in addition to referring to *the* Law, it is used for what we call a "right," that is, the kind of right that one person has against another. (As a legal right, this kind of right might be a legal capacity or a legal power.) In contrast to the first sense of *Recht*, in this sense, one can, indeed, speak of *ein Recht* ("a right") or, in the plural, of *Rechte* ("rights"). An analogous ambiguity is to be found in other Continental languages in such words as *jus* and *droit*, which may refer either to the corpus of law or to rights (as belonging to persons). For convenience in distinguishing these two senses of Right (*Recht, jus, droit*, and so on), Continental jurists have invented the expressions "objective Right" to designate the corpus of law and "subjective Right" to designate rights belonging to persons. Because this ambiguity is not present in English, *Recht* in the objective sense can be translated simply as "Law," and *Recht* in the subjective sense can be translated as "right." (There are, however, a few passages in the text where it is not entirely clear which sense of *Recht* is intended by Kant.)

Kant has his own way of dealing with this ambiguity of *Recht* (*jus*). When he wants to make it clear that he is referring to *Recht* in the objective sense, that is, as a corpus, he uses the term *Rechtslehre* ("jurisprudence").[9] In general, he uses the term *Lehre* for a corpus of principles, for example of laws. *Rechtslehre* and *Tugendlehre* are both bodies or systems of principles—the one legal, the other ethical—and they are not, as later uses of the word *Lehre* might suggest, theories or doctrines about these principles. (In my opinion, it is therefore not only unintelligible but also incorrect to refer to the present work as "The Doctrine of Right.")

The third and, for an understanding of Kant's philosophy, most important point about *Recht* is that this word, in contrast to our own word "law," carries with it the connotation of moral rightness. Indeed, for Kant, *Recht* applies *only* to

9 See, for example, pp. 43, 128.

the moral component of law in general. He expresses this by saying that *Recht* consists of a priori principles of practical reason. As such, it is the same for all men and equally binding on all. In this respect, *Recht* is to be distinguished from statutory law, the law of the land, which varies from country to country and can be known only by empirical means.[10]

In the traditional terms of Western political and legal philosophy, Kant's *Recht* is identical with what is generally known as natural law. The principal difference between Kant's view and that of other natural-law theorists is that, in his view, (1) our knowledge of *Recht* is a priori; (2) as law, it comes from within ourselves rather than from God or nature; and (3) the content differs somewhat.

Strictly speaking, then, Kant's *Recht* does not stand for law in general, but only for the right principles of law. To call it "law" at all is rather misleading. Therefore, I have usually translated it as "justice," by which I mean the principles of rectitude that are supposed to underlie law and politics.

Philosophers in the natural-law tradition commonly distinguish between what is universally right in itself (justice) and what is legally right for a particular locality (law). The former is called the natural law, and the latter, the positive law. Kant makes the same distinction, but usually prefers for the first the simple term *Recht* ("justice"), instead of *Naturrecht* ("natural law"). Instead of "positive law," he generally uses the term *öffentliche Gerechtigkeit* ("public justice") and sometimes *öffentliches Gesetz* ("public law"). These last two terms are used by him only to refer to law as it is promulgated and administered by a public authority, that is, to what is nowadays often known as "legal justice." Accordingly, in order to distinguish between *Recht* ("justice") and *Gerechtigkeit* in the translation, I have translated *Gerechtigkeit* as "legal justice." (It should be remembered that, for Kant,

[10] Kant often uses *Rechtens* for "law of the land," that is, the lawyer's law.

Gerechtigkeit, "legal justice," exists only where there are courts to administer justice.) [11]

To sum up, *Recht* (here translated "justice," "Law," "right") refers to what is right for all men and all places. It does not require any kind of enactment or recognition on the part of a political authority to establish its objective validity, for it is known a priori as a consequence of the categorical imperative. *Öffentliche Gerechtigkeit* (here translated "public justice") is what is administered by a judicial authority.

We can now understand Kant's general definition of justice (*Recht, Rechtslehre*) as the body of principles that can be made into external laws. What he means is that justice supplies the a priori principles of possible legislation and that the political authority makes and administers actual external laws in accordance with them (or should do so!).

Two questions arise immediately: First, what are these principles of justice? Second, what is the relation between theory and practice; that is, how much divergence between the demands of justice and actual legislation by political authorities is allowable? These are the two basic problems with which Kant is concerned in this work. I shall briefly discuss the first of these in the next section; and the second, in Section VII.

IV. Liberty and Coercion

Kant's doctrine of justice and law turns on the concept of coercion. Law is conceived as a coercive order, and justice treats only what can be made a matter of coercion (that is, an object of external legislation). The principles of justice themselves determine the legitimate and illegitimate uses of coercion. The legitimate use of coercion is coercion that accords

---

[11] I might point out that the English word "justice" contains an ambiguity that does not exist in German, for German has two words: *Recht,* for the body of principles, and *Gerechtigkeit,* for the administration and maintenance of what is just.

with liberty, and the illegitimate use is one that transgresses liberty. The illegitimate use of coercion is called violence.

Liberty (negative freedom) and violence are correlative opposites; where there is liberty there is no violence, and where there is violence there is no liberty. Man's innate right to liberty (freedom) consists in the right to be free from violence, and, indeed, all man's legal rights are derivable from this concept. Now, as already noted, the basis of man's right to liberty is the fact that he is an autonomous moral being, that is, a sovereign lawmaker, as well as a subject to the law (the moral law). In other words, it is his capacity for moral lawmaking that serves as an ethical foundation for his right to political liberty. It follows that this right to liberty is justified only as long as it is lawful. Lawfulness provides not only the basis but also the limits of rightful liberty.

Accordingly, any transgression of the bounds of lawful liberty is illegitimate. It is *ipso facto* an infringement of someone else's liberty, and, as such, is necessarily an act of violence. Violence is wrong, therefore, because it is an infringement of lawful liberty.

Coercion is, of course, permitted, but only if it is used to prevent violence or, more generally, to protect liberty. Otherwise, it is simply violence. The rightful function of the political order is to control violence and thus to protect liberty. Because everyone has the right to be protected from violence as an immediate consequence of his innate right to freedom, he also has a right to live under a political order and to demand that others join him in this. This political order, or civil society, as Kant calls it, is a necessary condition of the rule of law. The foundation of political authority, then, is man's innate right to live in peace and freedom, which, incidentally, includes his right to have his property secure and guaranteed. Everyone has a duty to obey the political authorities because they represent the rule of law, and, in obeying them, he is *ipso facto* respecting the rights of others to live in peace and freedom. Accordingly, it is the rule of law that provides the basis of political authority and political obedi-

ence, rather than, as for Locke, a presumed contractual relation among the citizens or between the people and the ruler.
(Kant doubts that such a contract ever took place and maintains that, even if it had taken place, it could not provide the
basis of political authority.)

Following earlier political theorists, Kant distinguishes between the state of nature (that is, a stateless society) and the
civil society (that is, a society subject to political authority).
Like Hobbes, Kant conceives the state of nature as one of
war, in the sense that, even when there is no overt aggression,
there is an ever-present threat of hostilities. It is not essential
to his theory to suppose that, as a matter of historical fact,
such a state of nature ever actually existed before the advent
of the civil society, although he does believe that in his era,
the nations of the world live in a state of nature in relation
to one another. The concept of the state of nature is introduced merely as a logical device to show in what way and to
what extent legal order depends on the state as such and, in
particular, to bring out the differences between our legal
duties to other individuals and our duties to the state.

A state of nature, being one of war and violence, is considered by Kant incompatible with man's innate right to liberty. In such a state, man does, of course, possess a kind of
lawless liberty, but he has no right thereto. His innate right
extends only to lawful liberty, because it comes from his
nature as a moral lawmaker. That is why it is a demand of
justice, incumbent on everyone, to quit the state of nature
and why everyone has a right to employ force to make others
join him in doing so. Thus, a lawful liberty to which everyone has a right is substituted for a lawless one to which no
one has a right.

War between states, as between individuals, is a condition
of lawlessness. Hence, the demand that one abandon the state
of nature applies to states as well as to individuals. On the
international level, it requires the establishment of a federa-
tion of states.[12]

12 See Kant, *Perpetual Peace*, trans. Lewis W. Beck, "Library of Liberal
Arts," No. 54 (New York: Liberal Arts Press, 1957).

Any act of violence or lawlessness, whether on the part of individuals or of states, represents a return to the state of nature and is to be deprecated as a crime of injustice. Hence, revolution, which Kant conceived as involving the dissolution of the civil state and a return to a state of nature, is always unjust. Treason and murder are crimes for the same reason.

Legitimate coercion—that is, coercion that is used to counterbalance illegitimate coercion (violence)—will on reflection be seen to be equivalent to coercion consistent with the freedom of everyone in accordance with universal laws. The principle that coercion is legitimate under these conditions explains why we can force others to quit the state of nature. It also explains the basis of the state's right and duty to punish criminals. Kant is very strict about punishment; no other end, such as deterrence or reformation, is allowed as a justification for punishment. The crime's being an act of violence, illegitimate coercion, provides both a sufficient and a necessary condition of the legitimate use of coercion—in this case, punishment.

These considerations concerning the conditions of legitimate coercion—namely, that it be used only to establish and preserve the rule of law—suggest that every state is limited in the kinds of coercion that it may employ. A state founded on violence, like the Nazi one, definitely exceeds those limits, and I do not see how Kant could, consistently with his stated principles, condemn those who opposed the activities of that kind of regime, although he repeatedly asserts that we must obey the powers that be.

The main function of the civil state is, therefore, to maintain the rule of law, to guarantee and protect the rights of its subjects. This he calls the juridical condition of society, the state of public justice, legal justice. The individual rights to be secured are not, however, themselves created by the civil society. They already exist in a state of nature, albeit only provisionally and not peremptorily. Hence, it is not the function of the state to create rights, but only to enforce them and to adjudicate disputes concerning them.

In sum, the doctrine of the state of nature is introduced by Kant, not to explain the historical origin of the civil state, but to exhibit the logical basis of various rights and duties of the individual. In particular, it makes plain two central theses of Kant's political theory: first, the unconditional demand for the rule of law as a prerequisite of peace and freedom and, second, the proposition that the basic rights of the individual are not created by the state, but are only protected by it.

V. Concepts of Roman Law Employed by Kant

The reader who is unfamiliar with Roman law may have some difficulty in understanding Kant's discussion of certain legal concepts that are not to be found in the Anglo-American system of common law. Let me therefore try to explain some of these concepts briefly.

A. *Private* versus *Public Law*. At the outset of Justinian's *Institutes*, a distinction is made between private law (*privatum jus*), as law that relates to the advantage of individuals, and public law (*publicum jus*), as law that relates to the welfare of the Roman state. In Roman law, private law encompasses the legal relations among individuals, the rights and duties of individuals with regard to other individuals. It includes the law of property, of contract, family law, and all the matters that are involved in civil actions. Public law, on the other hand, includes constitutional law, criminal law, and international law; in other words, that part of the law in which the state is involved as a party.

The distinction between two branches of the law forms the basis for the twofold division of the *Rechtslehre*. Kant's doctrine is that the basic principles of private law pertain provisionally in the state of nature and, in that sense, are logically independent of the state.

B. *Possession and Detention*. Roman law speaks of possession as a fact to be contrasted with ownership. One may possess something without owning it, for example, stolen goods, and one may own something without possessing it, for example, a thing that someone else has taken. Thus possession supposedly rests on a manifest fact, whereas ownership rests on a right of some kind.[13] The condition of fact, that is, the fact of physical custody or control, is called "detention" in Roman law. Kant regards the fact of detention as empirically ascertainable. Then, using his general distinction between phenomena (sensible) and noumena (intelligible), he undertakes to explain the distinction between possession and ownership (or property) in terms of two kinds of "possession," which he calls empirical and *de jure* possession (or "phenomenal" and "noumenal" possession—see section VI below).

C. *Property.* Kant does not use this word, but uses instead *das Meine, das Deine,* and *das Seine* (literally, what is "mine," "yours," and "his"). Because of the awkwardness of translating these terms, I have used "property" instead. By this is intended all of a person's assets, that is, his rights over both things and persons. This is a somewhat broader sense of "property" than is usually used in Anglo-American law, but the term is sometimes given this broader meaning in Roman law.[14] Roman law divides a man's property, i.e., his rights, into two kinds: rights *in rem* and rights *in personam.* Kant adds to these another kind, namely, rights *in rem* over persons.

D. *Rights* in rem versus *Rights* in personam. Under Roman law, a person may have two kinds of rights, rights over a thing (*in rem*) and rights against a person (*in personam*). Thus, if he owns a thing, for example, an automobile, then he has rights over that thing (*in rem*); if someone owes him something, then he has a right against that person (*in personam*). It is customarily said that rights *in rem* avail against the whole world, for example, one's rights over the automobile hold against everybody and anybody who might try to use it. Land

13 The Roman concept of possession is much more complicated than stated here, but for our purposes this characterization is sufficient. See Barry Nicholas, *Introduction to Roman Law* (Oxford: Oxford University Press, 1962), pp. 107–115.

14 See Charles Phineas Sherman, *Roman Law in the Modern World* (Boston: Boston Book Company, 1917), II, 157.

rights are typical cases of rights *in rem*. A right *in personam*, however, avails only against a specific person; for example, if someone owes me a debt, then my right holds only against that person and not against anyone else. Rights arising from contracts are typical cases of rights *in personam*.

E. *Rights* in rem *over Persons*. Kant thought that one of his most notable contributions to legal theory was the discovery of a third kind of right, namely, a right *in rem* over persons. The rights involved here might nowadays be more properly referred to as those involved in a legal status. Kant's examples are the rights of married persons over one another, of parents over children, and of masters over servants. These are obviously rights *over* persons, but they are at the same time rights that hold *against* the whole world, for example, the rights of noninterference. The main interest of this category for us is that it shows us how Kant goes about handling a concept that does not fit into the traditional categories. (The sections dealing with this are omitted in the present translation.)

VI. *Explanation of Some Technical Concepts in Kant's Philosophy*

Some brief remarks on a few of Kant's basic philosophical concepts may be helpful.

A. *Phenomena (Sensible) and Noumena (Intelligible)*. Throughout his philosophy, Kant relies on a distinction between two sorts of object of thought, namely, the objects with which empirical science is concerned and the objects with which ethics, theology, and politics are concerned. Phenomena (or sensible objects) are objects of empirical knowledge, exist in space and time, and come under the categories, for example, of temporal causality. In addition to phenomena, Kant maintains, we can think validly of other kinds of objects, "objects of the mere understanding," which are not empirical objects. Such nonphenomenal objects he calls "noumena" (intelligible objects). For our purposes, it is sufficient to point out that the objects of ethical, legal, and political thought, insofar as they are not matters of empirical knowledge, are noumena. The faculty that is principally concerned with these noumenal objects is called pure practical reason.

I find that, far from implying any mystical notions about supersensible realities, Kant simply means by "phenomenal" something like that which nowadays is called "descriptive" and, by "noumenal," that which is called "normative." Thus, judgments involving evaluations about what ought to be, being nonempirical, would be noumenal in Kant's sense. The opening discussion of the concept of property, § 1 of this work, illustrates this use of the phenomenal–noumenal distinction; there he distinguishes between two kinds of possession, namely, possession in the factual sense (sensible possession) and possession in the *de jure,* normative sense (intelligible possession). The latter may be called "property." [15]

The reader should be warned that, as Kant uses it, the distinction between these two kinds of thought, like the distinction between empirical and a priori, is not an absolute one. A careful reading of Kant will show, I think, that, when he characterizes the difference between two concepts in terms of the phenomenal–noumenal dichotomy, it is in order to bring out a significant logical difference between the particular concepts under discussion, rather than to assert an ontological or metaphysical thesis. Thus, for example, when he distinguishes between man as a phenomenon and man as a noumenon, he is directing our attention to two distinct ways of viewing him, each of which involves differing kinds of logical consequences, factual and evaluative.

B. *Wille* versus *Willkür.* Kant uses two words that can both properly be translated by the English word "will," namely, *der Wille* ("the Will," capitalized) and *die Willkür* ("the will," uncapitalized). These two words are direct translations of the Latin words *voluntas* and *arbitrium.*

Der Wille is used by Kant to stand for "will" when it functions as the source of a command. This sense of

15 See § 7, pp. 63–64.

"will" appears in sentences like "This is my Will," "The Will of the sovereign is law," and "Thy Will be done." Will is, in this sense, a legislating will. For Kant, it is the source of law, moral as well as legal. His conception of Will resembles closely Rousseau's conception of the general will, and, like that Will, it lays down the principles of right and wrong and cannot itself err. Moreover, because in Kant's system Will is identified with practical reason, the Will of each is the same as the Will of all, and its commands have universal validity.[16] It is clear, therefore, that, in Kant's theory of moral autonomy, the individual's Will plays the same role that is assigned to the Will of God by some theologians; it provides the foundation of morality.

Die Willkür ("will"), on the other hand, is the faculty of deciding, for example, to act. It may also be called "choice" or "arbitrary preference," for it selects between alternatives and is a reflection of the personal desires of the individual subject. Willkür, in contrast to Wille, is therefore individual-istic and arbitrary in the sense that what one person chooses often differs from and may even be incompatible with what is chosen by another. This kind of will provides the subject matter of law, for laws are concerned with directing and con-trolling the personal wills of individuals; that is, they deal with problems arising out of the conflicts of choices, prefer-ences, intentions, and decisions among men. The objects that are sought as objects of the will so described are called by Kant "the matter of the will."

The twin concepts of coercion and liberty (negative politi-cal freedom), which, as we have noted, are the principal con-cern of political philosophy, relate to the Willkür, not to the Wille, for liberty consists in being able to do what is in ac-cordance with one's will, whereas coercion means being forced against one's will (Willkür).

The relation between the two kinds of will is that der Wille is the legislative Will that issues decrees, as it were, for the

---

[16] Occasionally Kant speaks of a Privatwille ("private Will"). This kind of Will still functions to command or prescribe, but not universally.

Willkür, which acts or fails to act conformably with them. Nevertheless, the *Willkür* provides the subject matter and the occasion for such legislation. The distinction between these two senses of "will" is not always clearly and consistently drawn in Kant's writings, but it will suffice for our purposes if we note that the law originates in a Will but prescribes the relations between wills.[17]

C. *Deduction. Deduktion* ("Deduction," capitalized) is another technical concept in Kant's system and is not to be identified with "deduction" in the ordinary sense of "proof" or "demonstration." Kant compares the process of Deduction with a lawyer's vindicating a claim or a title; a Deduction aims at showing by what right we assert the principle at all. It is not a proof of the principle, since it is taken for granted that the principle itself is valid. A Deduction merely shows *how* the proposition in question is possible, that is, objectively valid.

In a general sense, the whole of the *Rechtslehre* might be described as a Deduction of the principles of justice and Law, that is, its aim is to show *how* and *why* they are valid, rather than to show *that* they are valid, for the principles themselves are never called into question nor are they ever proved in the strict sense of the term.

D. *Idea. Idee* ("Idea," capitalized) is another technical term in Kant's philosophy and is not to be confused with the English term "idea." Kant writes: "I understand by Idea a necessary concept of reason to which no corresponding object can be given in sense-experience." [18] As a "pure concept of reason," it is to be sharply distinguished from other kinds of concepts and ideas. An Idea is an archetype in the sense in which Plato's forms are archetypes. In fact, an Idea rep-

---

17 The word *Willkür* is not used in present-day German, although there is an adjective formed from it, *willkürlich,* meaning "arbitrary." For a more detailed discussion of these two concepts of will, see Lewis White Beck, *A Commentary on Kant's Critique of Practical Reason* (Chicago: The University of Chicago Press, 1960), pp. 176–181.

18 *Critique of Pure Reason,* trans. Norman Kemp Smith, A 327=B 383.

resents a certain kind of perfection that is not found in empirical reality, but which must be an object of our moral striving. (In Kant's view, therefore, it has practical rather than theoretical significance.)

Ideas are, in other words, ideals. There are many concepts that are referred to as Ideas in Kant's moral philosophy: God, freedom, and duty are called Ideas; and, in politics, the social contract, perpetual peace, and a republican form of government are referred to as Ideas. None of these are empirically real; they are real only in the sense that they are necessary objects of striving.

For example, when he speaks of the Idea of the state, he is not talking about any actual state or constitution, but only of the ideal toward which every state or constitution should strive:

> A constitution allowing *the greatest possible human freedom* in accordance with laws by which *the freedom of each is made to be consistent with that of all others* . . . is at any rate a necessary Idea, which must be taken as fundamental not only in first projecting a constitution but in all its laws. . . . This perfect state may never, indeed, come into being; none the less this does not affect the rightfulness of the Idea, which, in order to bring the legal organisation of mankind ever nearer to its greatest possible perfection, advances this maximum as an archetype.[19]

VII. The Ideal and the Actual in Kant's Political Philosophy

Every political philosophy must, sooner or later, come to grips with the issue of the relationship between the actual and the ideal in government and law. Should our allegiance be to what is actual or to what is ideal? Is law defined by what is actual or by what is ideal? The natural-law tradition, to which Kant unquestionably belongs, analyzes government and law by reference to the ideal. It maintains that law is part of

[19] *Ibid.*, A 316–317=B 373–374. Capitalized *I* in Idea, here and on the preceding page, is the present translator's addition.

morals. This has led to the frequent accusation that it utterly confuses crucial political issues by identifying law (and government) as it is with law (and government) as it ought to be. Legal positivists, who are the most ardent opponents of the natural-law theory, are quick to point out that the practical effect of identifying law with a part of morals is either to nullify existing law in favor of an ideal law or to elevate all existing law to the status of what is moral; in other words, the natural-law theorist, they maintain, has to be either a radical revolutionary or an unregenerate reactionary.

Kant himself was subjected to both criticisms even during his lifetime. Admittedly, at times he does seem to adopt extreme positions that appear to be incompatible with one another. The most notorious instance of this is his view concerning the French Revolution; he eulogizes this important event of his times as a "moral cause" inserting itself into history while (even on the same page!) condemning revolution as something that is always "unjust." [20]

However, a close study of the present work will show that, far from ignoring this seeming paradox, Kant makes it the central theme of his inquiry. The whole book may be regarded as an extended philosophical commentary on the relation between what is and what ought to be, both in politics and in law. In order to follow the various discussions in the book, it is essential to realize that at times he is discussing actual states and actual obligations, whereas at other times he is discussing the ideal. It is therefore necessary to explain how Kant conceives the relationship between them.

Let us begin with law. All laws—that is, positive laws—are based on the principles of justice, or natural Law. Therefore, we ought to obey them because they represent duties of justice. Nevertheless, some laws are obviously better than others, and there are, of course, also bad laws, that is, laws that ought not to have been made. Kant is ready to admit this and, indeed,

---

[20] "An Old Question Raised Again," trans. Robert E. Anchor in Kant, *On History*, ed. Lewis White Beck, "Library of Liberal Arts," No. 162 (New York: Library of Liberal Arts, 1963) pp. 143–146.

provides us with examples. In order to distinguish between laws as they are and laws as they ought to be, he calls the first "the letter of the law," and the second, "the spirit of the law." "The letter of the law" represents what is actual law and what must be obeyed; "the spirit of the law" represents what ought to be law and what we should strive for.

As far as government is concerned, Kant constantly emphasizes that some forms of government are better than others. A republican form of government, is, in his opinion, the best, that is, the most just form of government. By republican government he means a constitutional one in which there is a separation of powers into the legislative, executive, and judicial authorities. This form of government embodies the Idea of the state, that is, the concept of the state as it ought to be, although many, perhaps most, actual states are not republican in this sense.

The Idea of the state, the perfect constitution, derives from the Idea of the original contract, that is, the principle that government should ideally be by universal consent of its citizens.[21] In Kant's *Nachlass*—his posthumously published notes— the concept of the original contract is stated very clearly thus:

> The original contract is not a principle explaining the origin of the civil society; rather it is a principle explaining how it ought to be. . . . It is not the principle establishing the state; rather it is the principle of political government and contains the ideal of legislation, administration, and public legal justice.[22]

Every actual state represents to a greater or lesser degree of perfection the Idea of the state; in Plato's terms, it "participates in" or "imitates" the Idea of the state, the archetype. The quality of any actual state is measured by the degree to

[21] See Kant, *Perpetual Peace*, pp. 11–13.
[22] Kant, *Handschriftliche Nachlass*, VI, Band XIX of the *Gesammelte Schriften*, herausgegeben von der Preussischen Akademie der Wissenschaften (Berlin: Walter de Gruyter, 1934).

which it approaches the Idea; the closer to a republic it is, the better state it is. Progress consists in advancing toward the Idea. (That is why the French Revolution can be regarded as progress.)

All our political and legal obligations have their source in the Idea, and so we are obligated to obey the political authorities in actual states because, however imperfectly, they still represent the Idea.

There are two practical maxims that can be deduced from this conception of the Idea. First, there must never be any backward movement. Any course of action that is retrogressive, that is, leads from a better condition to a worse one, is *ipso facto* unjust. (For example, once a monarch has given up the sovereignty to the people, it would be unjust for them to give it back to him.) [23] The second maxim is that no step must be undertaken that would render further progress and the achievement of the Idea impossible. (For example, in war one must never do anything that would render peace impossible.) [24]

Finally, we encounter a typical Kantian argument for the proposition that the Idea is practically possible. Because we ought always to work for the realization of the Idea, it follows from the principle that ought implies can that the Idea is possible or, more accurately, that it is something that we must, for practical purposes, assume to be realizable. Thus we have a moral argument to give rational support to the hope that mankind can ultimately obtain a republican form of government and, on the international level, perpetual peace.

JOHN LADD

[23] See § 53.
[24] See § 57.

NOTE ON THE TEXT

The *Metaphysische Anfangsgründe der Rechtslehre*, Part I
of the *Metaphysik der Sitten,* was first published in 1797
(Königsberg, Friedrich Nicolovius). The second edition, which
contains an appendix, appeared in 1798, but there is some dispute concerning the extent to which Kant worked on it, for it
contains quite a few more errors than the first. The present
translation is based on Ernst Cassirer's edition, Volume VII of
Immanuel Kants Werke (Berlin, 1916).

Throughout, brackets indicate my own editorial interpola-
tions, including bracketed titles, in both the Table of Contents
and the text. Parenthetical remarks are uniformly Kant's.
Marginal numbers are the standard reference to Kantian works,
page numbers in the Königliche Preussische Akademie der
Wissenschaft edition (Berlin, 1902–1938), Volume VI.

I have tried to make this translation readable, intelligible,
and accurate. Kant's German is unusually difficult in this
work, and as a result, there are many passages where the translator has to depend on his own interpretation of Kant's thought
in order to make sense of them at all. I assume that anyone
who wishes to undertake a serious scholarly study of this work
will know German and be able to consult the text for himself.

Vocabulary presents another difficulty, since there are no
exact English equivalents for some of Kant's key terms. I therefore have often used different English expressions to translate
a single German word; but, in order to assure accuracy, I have
made it a rule never to use the same English expressions for
different German ones. It should be observed that certain English words are capitalized in order to indicate that they stand
for German words different from those translated by the
same English words when uncapitalized. (For details, see the
Glossary.)

The only previous translation of this work was by W. Hastie, B. D., under the title, *The Philosophy of Law* (Edinburgh, 1887). Hastie's translation is not only unreadable, but also highly inaccurate. There is a French translation by J. Tissot, entitled *Principes Metaphysiques du Droit* (Paris, 1837), and an Italian translation by Giovanni Vidari, entitled *La Dottrina del Diritto* (second edition, Torino, 1923). These last two translations are more accurate and more readable than Hastie's, and I have found them useful in interpreting obscure passages, although their interpretations were not always followed.

J. L.

SELECTED BIBLIOGRAPHY

General Works on Kant's Ethics

BECK, LEWIS WHITE. *A Commentary on Kant's Critique of Practical Reason.* Chicago: The University of Chicago Press, 1960.

COPLESTON, FREDERICK. *A History of Philosophy.* Vol. VI, Part II, "Kant." Garden City, New York: Doubleday & Company, 1964.

GREGOR, M. J. *Laws of Freedom, a Study of Kant's Method of Applying the Categorical Imperative in the* Metaphysik der Sitten. Oxford: Basil Blackwell, 1963.

WICK, WARNER. Introduction, "Kant's Moral Philosophy," in Kant, *The Metaphysical Principles of Virtue.* Trans. JAMES ELLINGTON. "Library of Liberal Arts," No. 85. New York: Liberal Arts Press, 1964.

Works Relating to Kant's Political and Legal Philosophy

ARMSTRONG, A. C. "Kant's Philosophy of Peace and War," *Journal of Philosophy,* XXVIII (1931), 197–204.

BECK, LEWIS WHITE. Translator's Introduction, in Kant, *Perpetual Peace.* "Library of Liberal Arts," No. 54. New York: Liberal Arts Press, 1957.

———. "Les deux concepts kantiens du vouloir dans leur contexte politique," *Annales de philosophie politique,* IV (1962), 119–137. "Kant's Two Conceptions of the Will in Their Political Context," in Beck, *Studies in the Philosophy of Kant.* New York: Liberal Arts Press, 1965.

———. Editor's Introduction, in Kant, *On History.* "Library of

Liberal Arts," No. 162. New York: Liberal Arts Press, 1963.

BOURKE, JOHN. "Kant's Doctrine of 'Perpetual Peace,'" *Philosophy*, XVII (1942), 324–333.

BROWN, STUART M., JR. "Has Kant a Philosophy of Law?" *Philosophical Review*, LXXXI (1961), 33–48.

BUCHDA, GERHARD. *Das Privatrecht Immanuel Kants*. Inaugural dissertation, University of Jena, 1929.

CAIRNS, HUNTINGTON. *Legal Philosophy from Plato to Hegel*. Chapter XII, "Kant." Baltimore: Johns Hopkins Press, 1949.

FRIEDRICH, C. J. *Inevitable Peace*. Cambridge, Mass.: Harvard University Press, 1948.

——. *The Philosophy of Law in Historical Perspective*. Chapter XIV, "Law as the Expression of the General Will, Rousseau and Kant." 2nd ed. Chicago: The University of Chicago Press, 1963.

HAENSEL, WERNER. *Kants Lehre vom Widerstandsrecht*. Kant-Studien, No. 60. Berlin, 1926.

HANCOCK, R. N. "Kant's Political Philosophy." Unpublished dissertation, Yale University, 1956.

LISSER, KURT. *Der Begriff des Rechts bei Kant*. Kant-Studien, No. 58. Berlin, 1922.

REISS, H. S. "Kant and the Right to Rebellion," *Journal of the History of Ideas*, XVII (1956), 179–192.

SCHWARZ, WOLFGANG. "Kant's Philosophy of Law and International Peace," *Philosophy and Phenomenological Research*, XXIII (1962), 71–80.

THE METAPHYSICS OF MORALS

Preface to Part I
The Metaphysical Elements of Justice

Introduction

PREFACE

The *Critique of Practical Reason* was to be followed by a system, *The Metaphysics of Morals*. *The Metaphysics of Morals* falls into two parts: *The Metaphysical Elements of Justice* and *The Metaphysical Elements of Virtue*. (They may be considered the counterparts of *The Metaphysical Elements of Natural Science*,[1] which has already been published.) The following introductory remarks are intended to describe and, in part, to elucidate the form of this system.

The theory of justice, which constitutes the first part of the theory of morals, is the kind of theory from which we demand a system derived from reason. Such a system might be called "the metaphysics of justice." Because, however, the concept of justice is a pure concept which at the same time also takes practice (i.e., the application of the concept to particular cases presented in experience) into consideration, it follows that, in making a subdivision [of its concepts], a metaphysical system of justice would have to take into account the empirical diversity and manifoldness of those cases in order to be complete in its subdivision (and completeness in its subdivisions is an indispensable requirement of a system of reason). Completeness in the subdivision of the empirical [i.e., of empirical concepts] is, however, impossible, and, when it is attempted (or when even an approach to completeness is attempted), such concepts do not belong to the system as integral parts of it, but are introduced by way of examples in the annotations. Thus, the only appropriate name for the first part of the theory of morals is *The Metaphysical Elements of Justice*, for, if we take these cases of application into account, we can ex-

1 [*Metaphysische Anfangsgründe der Naturwissenschaft* (Riga, 1786). This work is devoted to an exposition of various a priori principles of natural science, in particular of Newtonian mechanics. (An English translation will be published in the Library of Liberal Arts Series, 1966.)]

pect to attain only an approximation of a system, not a system itself. Accordingly, the same method of exposition that was used in the (earlier) *Metaphysical Elements of Natural Science* will be adopted here; the discussion of justice so far as it belongs to the outline of an a priori system will appear in the main text, whereas the discussion of those rights that are related to particular cases arising in experience will appear in the annotations, which are sometimes rather lengthy. Unless some such procedure is adopted, the parts that are concerned with metaphysics will not be clearly distinguishable from the parts that refer to the empirical practice of Law.[2]

206

I have often been reproached for writing in a philosophical style that is obscure; indeed, I have even been charged with intentionally cultivating and affecting unclarity in order to give the appearance of having had deep insights. There is no better way of anticipating or removing this objection than by readily accepting the duty that Herr Garve,[3] a philosopher in the true sense, has laid down as especially incumbent on any philosophical writer. Nevertheless, in accepting this duty, I would limit it to the condition that it must be obeyed only to the extent that is allowed by the nature of the science that is to be improved and enlarged.

This wise man (in his "Miscellaneous Essays"[4]) quite rightly demands that every philosophical theory be capable of being popularized (that is, that it must be possible to make it intelligible to the general public) if the author of the theory himself is to avoid being charged with conceptual obscurity. I admit this gladly, with the exception only of the system of a critique of the faculty of reason itself and of everything that depends solely on this system for its determination. My reason for this is that the distinction between the sensible and the supersensible in our knowledge still comes under the competence of reason. This system can never become popular, nor can, in general, any formal metaphysics, although their results

[2][*Rechtspraxis*. For the translation of *Recht*, see Introduction, pp. xv–xvii.]

[3] [Christian Garve (1742–1798), professor of philosophy at Leipzig.]

[4] [*Vermischte Aufsätze* (Breslau, 1796), pp. 352 ff.]

can be rendered quite illuminating for the ordinary man (who is a metaphysician without knowing it!). In this subject, popularity (popular language) is unthinkable; instead, we have to insist on scholastic precision (for this is the language of the schools), even if it is denounced as meticulosity. Only by this means can over-hasty reason be brought to understand itself before it makes its dogmatic assertions.

When, however, pedants presume to address the general public (from the pulpit or in popular writings) using the kind of technical vocabulary that is suitable only for the schools, the critical philosopher should not be blamed any more than the grammarian should be blamed for the follies of the word-caviler (*logodaedalus*). The laughter should be turned against the man only, not the science.

It sounds arrogant, egotistical, and, to those who have not yet given up their ancient philosophical system, derogatory to assert that before the advent of critical philosophy there was no philosophy. Before we can pass judgment on this apparent 207 presumption, we must first ask: Is it indeed possible for there to be more than a single philosophy? Certainly there have been various ways of philosophizing and of going back to the first principles of reason in order to lay, with greater or less success, the foundations of a system. Not only have there been, but there also had to be many attempts of this kind, each of which also deserves credit from contemporary philosophy. Nevertheless, inasmuch as there is, objectively speaking, still only one human reason, there cannot be many philosophies; that is, however variously, even contradictorily, men may have philosophized over one and the same proposition, only a single system of philosophy founded on principles is possible. Thus, the moralist says quite rightly: There is only one virtue and one theory of virtue, that is, a single system that unites all the duties of virtue under one principle. The chemist says: There is only one [system of] chemistry (that of Lavoisier).[5]

---

[5] [Antoine Laurent Lavoisier (1743–1794), French chemist, finally refuted the phlogiston theory in chemistry and laid the foundations for modern chemistry.]

Likewise, the physician says: There is only one principle for the system of classifying diseases (that of Brown).[6] But the fact that the new system has superseded all the others does not detract from the merit of earlier men (moralists, chemists, and physicians), because, without their discoveries or even without their unsuccessful attempts, we should never have attained the systematic unity of the true principle of all philosophy.

When, therefore, someone announces a system of philosophy as his own creation, he is in effect saying that there has been no other philosophy prior to his. For, were he to admit that there is another (and true) philosophy, then he would be admitting that there are two different philosophies concerning the same thing, and that would be self-contradictory. Consequently, when the critical philosophy announces that it is a philosophy prior to which there was absolutely no philosophy, it is not doing anything different from what anyone who constructs a philosophy according to his own plan has done, will do, and, indeed, must do.

Of less significance, but not entirely without importance, is the reproach that one essential and distinctive part of this philosophy is not a product of its own inner development, but has been taken from another philosophy (or mathematics). An example of this is the discovery that a reviewer from Tübingen [7] claims to have made concerning the definition of philosophy that the author of the *Critique of Pure Reason* gives out as his own, not inconsiderable, contribution. He finds that this definition was given in practically the same words by someone else many years ago.[8] I will leave it to the reader to decide

208

6 [John Brown (1735–1788), Scottish physician. His *Elementa Medicinae* (1780) was much in vogue at the time.]

7 [Probably Prof. J. F. Flatt, who reviewed many of Kant's works in the *Tübingen Gelehrter Anzeiger.*]

8 Porro de actuali constructione hic non quaeritur, cum ne possint quidem sensibiles figurae ad rigorem definitionum effingi; sed requiritur cognitio eorum, quibus absolvitur formatio, quae intellectualis quaedam constructio est—C. A. Hausen, *Elem. Mathes.* (1743), Part I, p. 86. ["Furthermore, the concern here is not with the actual construction, for sensible figures cannot be made with the rigor required by a definition; rather,

whether the words *intellectualis quaedam constructio* were
meant to express the thought of "the exhibition of a given
concept in an a priori intuition" through which philosophy is
once and for all quite definitely distinguished from mathematics. I am certain that Hausen himself would have refused
to accept this interpretation of his words. Indeed, the possibility of an a priori intuition and of space being such an
intuition, rather than merely (as Wolff held [9]) the juxtaposi-
tion of the manifold of objects external to one another that
is given in empirical intuition—all this would have thoroughly
shocked him for the simple reason that he would have felt that
a consideration of such questions would entangle him in
far-reaching philosophical investigations. By the words "the
exhibition [construction] made, as it were, by the understanding," this acute mathematician meant simply that, in an (empirical) drawing of a line corresponding to a concept, we pay
attention only to the rule [by which it is constructed], and we
ignore and abstract from the deviations from a perfect line
that cannot be avoided when we make a drawing; his point
can easily be seen if we think of the construction of figures
in geometry that are supposed to be equal to one another
[*Gleichung*].

Least significant of all from the point of view of the spirit of
this critical philosophy is the mischief wrought by its imita-
tors, who have made improper use of the technical expressions
of the *Critique of Pure Reason*. In the *Critique,* these expressions cannot very well be easily replaced by others, but they
should not be used outside this philosophical context in the
public interchange of ideas. This mischief certainly deserves
to be corrected, as Herr Nicolai [10] has done, although he

---

the knowledge that is sought is of what produces the form of the figure,
which is, as it were, a construction of the intellect"—C. A. Hausen (1693–
1745), professor of mathematics at Leipzig.]

[9] [Christian Wolff (1674–1754), in his *Ontology,* § 588.]

[10] [Christoph Friedrich Nicolai (1733–1811), German author and book-
seller. He belonged to a group calling themselves "popular philosophers"
and made ridiculous attacks on the ideas of Kant, Goethe, Schiller, and
others. The present reference is to *Die Geschichte eines dicken Mannes*

avoids asserting that these expressions can be entirely dispensed with even in their proper field, as though they were used everywhere as a cover to hide a poverty of thought. In the meantime, of course, it is more fun to laugh at the unpopular pedant than at an uncritical ignoramus. (Actually, a metaphysician who rigidly adheres to his system without turning to a critique belongs to this latter class, although he deliberately ignores those considerations that he will not allow because they are not part of the system of his old school.) But if, as Shaftesbury says, a touchstone—which is not to be despised—for the truth of a theory (especially a practical one) is that it survives being laughed at,[11] then, indeed, the turn of the critical philosopher will come in time, and he will be able to laugh last, and therefore also best, when he sees the systems of those who have talked big for such a long time collapse like houses of cards and sees all their adherents run off and disappear—a fate that inevitably awaits them.

Toward the end of the book, I have worked out some of the sections in less detail than might be expected in comparison to the earlier ones. This is partly because it seemed to me that they could be easily inferred from the earlier statements and partly because the subjects of the later parts (concerning public Law) are just now under so much discussion and are yet so important that they amply justify delaying for a while the making of any decisive pronouncements.

I hope that *The Metaphysical Elements of Virtue* will be ready shortly.[12]

209

("The Story of a Fat Man") (Berlin and Stettin, 1794), where he tries to make fun of the use of Kantian terminology in everyday life. This probably explains Kant's bitter remarks about laughing at philosophers.]

11 [Anthony Ashley Cooper, Third Earl of Shaftesbury (1671–1713), in his *Characteristics of Men, Manners, Opinions, Times,* Treatise II, "*Sensus Communis;* An Essay on the Freedom of Wit and Humour" (1709), Part I, section 1, paragraph 3: "Truth . . . may bear all lights; and one of those principal lights . . . is ridicule itself. . . . So much, at least, is allowed by all who at any time appeal to this criterion."]

12 [This sentence was omitted from the second edition. The second part of the *Metaphysics of Morals* appeared during the same year (1797).]

Table of the
Division of the Theory of Justice

FIRST PART

Private Law in Regard to External Objects
(The Body of Those Laws That Do Not Require
External Promulgation)

FIRST CHAPTER
Of the Mode of Having Something External as One's Property

SECOND CHAPTER
Of the Mode of Acquiring Something External

Division of External Acquisition
FIRST SECTION
Rights *in rem*
SECOND SECTION
Rights *in personam*
THIRD SECTION
Rights *in rem* over Persons
EPISODIC SECTION
Of Ideal Acquisition

THIRD CHAPTER
Of Subjectively Stipulated Acquisition Before a Judiciary

SECOND PART
Public Law
(The Body of Laws Requiring Public Promulgation)

FIRST SECTION
Municipal Law
SECOND SECTION
The Law of Nations
THIRD SECTION
World Law

INTRODUCTION TO THE
METAPHYSICS OF MORALS

I

OF THE RELATION OF THE FACULTIES OF
THE HUMAN MIND TO THE MORAL LAWS

The faculty of desire is the capacity to be the cause of the objects of one's representations by means of these representations. The capacity that a being has of acting in accordance with its representations is *life*.

First, desire or aversion always involve pleasure or displeasure, and the susceptibility to pleasure or displeasure is called *feeling*. But the converse does not always hold, for there can be a pleasure that does not involve any desire for an object, but merely the representation that one frames for himself of an object (it does not matter whether the object of this representation actually exists). Second, the pleasure or displeasure taken in an object of desire does not always precede the desire and cannot always be regarded as the cause of it, but must sometimes be regarded as its effect.

Now, the ability to take pleasure or displeasure in a representation is called feeling because both pleasure and displeasure involve what is merely subjective in relation to our representation and do not refer to an object as an object of possible knowledge [1] (not even to the knowledge of our own

---

[1] Sensibility can in general be defined by means of the subjective element in our representations, for it is the understanding that first refers the representations to an object; that is, it alone thinks something by means of them. Now, the subjective element in our representations may be of two kinds. On the one hand, it can be referred to an object as a means to cognizing it (with regard either to its form or to its matter; in the first case, it is called pure intuition and, in the second, sensation); here sensibility, as the receptivity for a representation that is thought, is sense. On the other hand, the subjective element in our representations

10

state). In other cases, however, sensations, in addition to the 212
quality that depends on the constitution of the subject (for
example, the quality of red, of sweet, and so on), also are referred to objects and constitute part of our knowledge. But
pleasure or displeasure (in what is red or sweet) expresses absolutely nothing in the object, but simply a relation to the
subject. Pleasure and displeasure cannot be more closely defined for the reason just given. We can only specify their consequence under certain circumstances in order to make them
recognizable in use.

Pleasure that is necessarily connected with desire (for an object whose representation affects feeling in this way) may be
called *practical pleasure,* whether it is the cause or the effect
of the desire. On the other hand, pleasure that is not necessarily connected with a desire for an object and that essentially, therefore, is not pleasure taken in the existence of the
object of the representation, but only adheres to the mere
representation, can be called mere *contemplative pleasure,* or
passive gratification. [The ability to have] the feeling of the
latter kind of pleasure is called *taste.* In a practical philosophy, accordingly, this kind of pleasure can be treated only incidentally, not as a concept properly belonging to that philosophy. But, as regards practical pleasure, the determination
of the faculty of desire that is caused by and, accordingly, is
necessarily preceded by this pleasure is called *appetite* in the
strict sense; habitual appetite, however, is called *inclination.*
The connection of pleasure with the faculty of desire, insofar
as this connection is judged by the understanding to be valid
according to a general rule (though only for the subject), is
called *interest;* and hence in this case the practical pleasure is

---

may be such that it cannot become a factor in cognition inasmuch as it
contains only the relation of a representation to the subject and does not
contain anything that can be used for cognizing the object; in this case,
the receptivity for the representation is called feeling. Now, feeling contains the effect of the representation (whether it be a sensible or an intellectual representation) on the subject and belongs to sensibility, even
though the representation itself may belong to the understanding or to
reason.

an interest of inclination. On the other hand, if the pleasure can follow only upon an antecedent determination of the faculty of desire, then it is an intellectual pleasure; and the interest in the object must be called an interest of reason. If the interest were sensible and not founded merely on pure principles of reason, then sensation would have to be joined with pleasure and so be able to determine the faculty of desire. Although where a merely pure interest of reason must be assumed, no interest of inclination can be attributed to it; nevertheless, in order to accommodate ourselves to ordinary speech, we may admit an inclination even to what can only be the object of an intellectual pleasure, that is to say, a habitual desire from a pure interest of reason. Such an inclination would, however, be not the cause but the effect of a pure interest of reason; we could call it *sense-free inclination* (*propensio intellectualis*).

Further, *concupiscence* (lusting after something) is to be distinguished from desire itself as being the stimulus to its determination. Concupiscence is always a sensible mental state that has not yet turned into an act of the faculty of desire.

The faculty of desiring in accordance with concepts is called the faculty of doing or forbearing as one likes [*nach Belieben zu tun oder zu lassen*] insofar as the ground determining it to action is found in the faculty of desire itself and not in the object. Insofar as it is combined with the consciousness of the capacity of its action to produce its object, it is called *will*, or *Choice* [*Willkür*]; [2] if not so combined, its act is called a *wish*. The faculty of desire whose internal ground of determination and, consequently, even whose likings [*das Belieben*] are found in the reason of the subject is called the *Will* [*der Wille*].[3] Accordingly, the Will is the faculty of desire regarded not, as is will, in its relation to action, but rather in its relation to the ground determining will to action. The Will itself has no determining ground; but, insofar as it can determine will, it is practical reason itself.

[2] [See Translator's Introduction, p. xxvi.]
[3] [See Translator's Introduction, pp. xxv–xxvii.]

Insofar as reason can determine the faculty of desire in general, will and even mere wish may be included under Will. A will that can be determined by pure reason is called free will. A will that is determined only by inclination (sensible impulse, *stimulus*) would be animal will (*arbitrium brutum*). Human will, on the other hand, is the kind of will that is affected but not determined by impulses. Accordingly, in itself (apart from an acquired facility with reason), it is not pure; but it can nevertheless be determined to actions by pure Will. Freedom of will is just the aforementioned independence from determination by sensible impulses; this is the negative concept of freedom. The positive concept of freedom is that of the capacity of pure reason to be of itself practical. Now, this is possible only through the subjection of the maxim of every action to the condition of its fitness to be a universal law. Inasmuch as pure reason is applied to will without regard to the object of will, it is the faculty of principles (and here they are practical principles, and so it is a legislative faculty); and, as such, because it does not contain the matter of the law, there is nothing that it can make the supreme law and determining ground of will except the form of the law, which consists in the fitness of the maxim of will to be a universal law. Because maxims of man that are based on subjective causes do not of themselves coincide with the aforementioned objective maxims, reason can only prescribe this law as an imperative of command or prohibition.

214

In contradistinction to natural laws, these laws of freedom are called *moral* laws. Insofar as they are directed to mere external actions and their legality, they are called *juridical;* but when, in addition, they demand that these laws themselves be the determining grounds of actions, then they are *ethical*. Accordingly we say: agreement with juridical laws constitutes the *legality* of action, whereas agreement with ethical ones constitutes its *morality*. The freedom to which juridical laws refer can only be freedom in its external exercise; but the freedom to which ethical laws refer is freedom in both the internal and external exercise of will, insofar as will is determined by laws of reason. So in theoretical philosophy we say that only the objects of the outer senses are in space, whereas all objects—those of the outer senses as well as those of the inner sense—are in time, inasmuch as the representations of both kinds of object are still representations and therefore belong to inner sense.[4] Similarly, whether we consider freedom in the external or in the internal exercise of will, freedom's laws, being pure practical laws of reason governing free Will in general, must at the same time be internal grounds of determination of will, although these laws may not always be considered from this point of view.

II

OF THE IDEA AND THE NECESSITY OF A METAPHYSICS OF MORALS

It has been shown elsewhere [5] that we must have a priori principles for natural science, which has to do with the objects of the outer senses, and that it is possible—indeed, even necessary—to prefix a system of such principles, under the name of a metaphysical natural science, to physics, which is natural science applied to particular experiences. Metaphysical natural science, if it is to be universal in the strict sense, must be deduced from a priori grounds; although physics (at least when the purpose is to guard its propositions against error) may assume many principles to be universal on the testimony of experience, just as Newton adopted the principle of the equality of action and reaction in the influence of bodies on one another as based on experience and yet extended that principle to all material nature. The chemists go still further and base their most general laws of combination and dissociation of substances by their own forces entirely on experience, and yet they have such confidence in the universality and

4 [Kant's doctrine of outer and inner sense is expounded in his *Critique of Pure Reason*, A 23 = B 37 *et passim*.]

5 [Namely, in the *Metaphysische Anfangsgründe der Naturwissenschaft* (*Metaphysical Elements of Natural Science*) (1786).]

necessity of these laws that they do not worry about discovering any error in the experiments that they make with them.

But it is otherwise with moral laws. They are valid as laws only insofar as they can be seen to have an a priori basis and to be necessary. Indeed, concepts and judgments concerning ourselves and our actions and omissions have no moral significance at all if they contain only what can be learned from experience. Anyone so misled as to make into a basic moral principle something derived from this source would be, in danger of the grossest and most pernicious errors.

If moral philosophy were nothing but eudaemonism [the happiness-theory], it would be absurd to look to a priori principles for help. However plausible it might seem that reason, even before experience, could discern by what means one can attain a lasting enjoyment of the true joys of life, nevertheless everything that is taught a priori on this subject is either tautological or assumed without any ground. Only experience can teach us what brings us joy. The natural drives for food, sex, rest, movement, and (in the development of our natural predispositions) for honor, the enlargement of our knowledge, and so on, can alone teach us where to find these joys and can only do so for each individual in his own way and, similarly, can teach him the means by which to seek them. All apparently a priori reasoning is here basically nothing but experience raised to generality through induction; this generality (*secundum principia generalia, non universalia*) [6] is so deficient that infinitely many exceptions must be allowed everyone in order to make his choosing [*Wahl*] of a way of life fit his particular inclination and susceptibility to satisfaction; still, in the end he becomes prudent only through his own or other people's misfortunes.

216

But it is otherwise with the instructions of morality. They command everyone without regard to his inclinations, solely because and insofar as he is free and has practical reason. Instruction in the laws of morality is not drawn from observation of oneself and the animality within him nor from the per-

[6] ["According to general principles, but not universal ones."]

ception of the course of the world as to how things happen and how men in fact do act (although the German word *Sitten*, like the Latin word *mores*, designates only manners and ways of life). But reason commands how one ought to act, even though no instance of such action might be found; moreover, reason does not take into consideration the advantage that can accrue to us therefrom, which admittedly only experience could teach us. Although reason allows us to seek our advantage in every way open to us and can, on the basis of the testimony of experience, also probably promise us greater advantages, on the average, from obeying its commands than from transgressing them, especially if obedience is accompanied by prudence, yet the authority of its precepts as commands does not rest on this fact. Instead, reason uses such considerations (by way of advice) only as counterweights to inducements to do the opposite of what is moral; as counterweights they are used, first, to correct the error due to partiality in the scales of practical judgment and, then, to make certain that the scales are tipped in favor of the a priori grounds of a pure practical reason.

If, therefore, a system of a priori knowledge from mere concepts is called *metaphysics*, then a practical philosophy that has as its object not nature but the freedom of will, will presuppose and require a metaphysics of morals; that is, to have such a metaphysics is itself a duty. Moreover, every man has such a metaphysics within himself, although commonly only in an obscure way; for, without a priori principles, how could he believe that he has a universal legislation within himself? Just as, in the metaphysics of nature, there must be principles for the application of those supreme universal basic principles of nature in general to objects of experience, so likewise a metaphysics of morals cannot dispense with similar principles of application. Accordingly, we shall often have to take as our object the special nature of man, which can be known only by experience, in order to show the implications of the universal moral principles for human nature. But this will not detract from the purity of such laws or cast any doubt

217

on their a priori origin; that is to say, a metaphysics of morals cannot be founded on anthropology, although it can be applied to it.

The counterpart of a metaphysics of morals, as the other member of the division of practical philosophy in general, would be moral anthropology, which would, however, contain only the subjective conditions in human nature hindering as well as favoring the execution of the laws of the metaphysics of morals. It would treat of the engendering, propagation, and strengthening of basic moral principles (in education through school and popular instruction) and other like doctrines and precepts based on experience, which cannot be dispensed with but which must by no means come before the metaphysics or be mixed with it. Otherwise, one would run the risk of eliciting erroneous or at least indulgent moral laws. Such laws would falsely portray as unattainable that which has merely not yet been attained, either because the law has not been discerned and set forth in its purity (the very thing in which its strength consists) or because spurious or impure incentives are used for what in itself accords with duty and is good. Such incentives leave us no certain basic moral principles to serve either as guides to judgment or for the discipline of the mind in its obedience to duty, whose precept must absolutely be given only a priori by pure reason.

The higher division under which that just mentioned [7] comes is the division of philosophy into theoretical and practical. I have explained myself sufficiently concerning this elsewhere (in the *Critique of Judgment* [8]) and have shown that the latter branch can be nothing but worldly wisdom. Everything practical that is supposed to be possible according to laws of nature (the proper business of technical skill [*Kunst*] [9]) depends for its concept entirely on the theory of nature. Only that which is practical in accordance with laws of freedom can

7 [That is, metaphysics of morals and moral anthropology.]

8 [Introduction, sections I and II.]

9 [This is obviously a German translation of the Greek *technē*—art— that plays such a central role in Plato's *Republic*.]

have principles that do not depend on any [scientific] theory, for there can be no [scientific] theory of that which transcends the determination of nature. Accordingly, by the practical part of philosophy (coordinate with its theoretical part) is to be understood not any technically practical, but, rather, a morally practical discipline [*Lehre*]. And if will's ability [*Fertigkeit der Willkür*] to act in accordance with laws of freedom —in contrast to laws of nature—is also to be called skill here, then such a skill must be understood as one making possible a system of freedom that would be like a system of nature. It would be, in truth, a divine skill if we were in a position, by means of such a skill, to fulfill completely the precepts of reason and to carry the Idea [10] thereof into execution.

218

III

OF THE SUBDIVISION OF A METAPHYSICS OF MORALS [11]

All legislation (whether it prescribes internal or external actions, and these either a priori through mere reason or through another person's will) consists of two elements: first, a law that objectively represents the action that is to be done as necessary, that is, that makes the action a duty; second, an incentive that subjectively links the ground determining will to this action with the representation of the law. So this sec-

---

[10] [See Translator's Introduction, pp. xxvii–xxviii.]

[11] The Deduction * of the division of a system, that is, the proof of its completeness as well as of its continuity, namely, that the transition from the concept being divided to each member of the division in the whole series of subdivisions takes place without any gaps (*divisio per saltum*), is one of the most difficult conditions for the constructor of a system to fulfill. It is even difficult to say what is the ultimate divided concept of which right and wrong (*aut fas aut nefas*) are divisions. It is the act of free will in general. Similarly, teachers of ontology begin with the concepts of something and nothing without being aware that these are already subdivisions of a concept that is not given but that can only be the concept of an object in general.

* [See Translator's Introduction, p xxvii.]

ond element amounts to this, that the law makes duty the incentive. Through the former element, the action is represented as a duty; as such, it is mere theoretical knowledge of the possible determination of will, that is, a knowledge of practical rules. Through the latter element, the obligation so to act is combined in the subject with a determining ground of will in general.

Therefore (even though one legislation may agree with another with regard to actions that are required as duties; for example, the actions might in all cases be external ones) all **219** legislation can nevertheless be differentiated with regard to the incentives. If legislation makes an action a duty and at the same time makes this duty the incentive, it is *ethical*. If it does not include the latter condition in the law and therefore admits an incentive other than the Idea of duty itself, it is *juridical*. As regards juridical legislation, it is easily seen that the incentive here, being different from the Idea of duty, must be derived from pathological grounds determining will, that is, from inclinations and disinclinations and, among these, specifically from disinclinations, since it is supposed to be the kind of legislation that constrains, not an allurement that invites.

The mere agreement or disagreement of an action with the law, without regard to the incentive of the action, is called *legality;* but, when the Idea of duty arising from the law is at the same time the incentive of the action, then the agreement is called the *morality* of the action.

Duties in accordance with juridical legislation can be only external duties because such legislation does not require that the Idea of this duty, which is internal, be of itself the ground determining the will of the agent. Because such legislation still requires a suitable incentive for the law, it can combine only external incentives with the law. On the other hand, ethical legislation also makes internal actions duties, but does not, however, exclude external actions; rather, it applies generally to everything that is a duty. But, for the very reason that ethical legislation includes in its law the internal incentive of the action (the Idea of duty), which is a determination that must by no means be mixed with external legislation, ethical legislation cannot be external (not even the external legislation of a divine Will), although it may adopt duties that rest on external legislation and take them, insofar as they are duties, as incentives in its own legislation.

From this it can be seen that all duties, simply because they are duties, belong to Ethics.[12] But their legislation is not therefore always included under Ethics; in the case of many duties, it is quite outside Ethics. Thus, Ethics commands me to fulfill my pledge given in a contract, even though the other party could not compel me to do so; but the law (*pacta sunt servanda* [13]) and the duty corresponding to it are taken by Ethics from jurisprudence. Accordingly, the legislation that promises must be kept is contained in *jus* [14] and not in Ethics. Ethics teaches only that, if the incentive that juridical legislation combines with that duty, namely, external coercion, were absent, the Idea of duty alone would still be sufficient as an incentive. If this were not so and if the legislation itself were not juridical and the duty arising from it thus not properly a duty of justice (in contradistinction to a duty of virtue), then keeping faith (in accordance with one's promise in a contract) would be put in the same class with actions of benevolence and the manner in which we are bound to perform them as a duty, and this certainly must not happen. It is not a duty of virtue to keep one's promise, but a duty of justice, one that we can be coerced to perform. Nevertheless, it is a virtuous action (proof of virtue) to do so where no coercion is to be feared. Jurisprudence and ethics [*Rechtslehre* and *Tugend-*

220

----

12 [*Ethik* is translated "Ethics," with a capital *E;* "ethics" is the translation of *Tugendlehre.* For the most part, Kant uses these terms interchangeably.]

13 ["Agreements ought to be kept."]

14 ["Right," "Law," "justice." This is the word that Kant translates *Rechtslehre* ("jurisprudence"). He uses *jus* here and *Recht* ("justice") later in the paragraph instead of *Rechtslehre* because these two nouns are of neuter gender, and, in his typical style, Kant wants to draw the distinction grammatically as well.]

lehre] are distinguished, therefore, not so much by their differing duties as by the difference in the legislation that combines one or the other incentive with the law.

Ethical legislation is that which cannot be external (though the duties may be external); juridical legislation is that which can also be external. Thus, to keep one's promise in a contract is an external duty; but the command to do so merely because it is a duty, without regard to any other incentive, belongs only to internal legislation. Accordingly, this obligation is reckoned as belonging to Ethics, not as being a special kind of duty (a special kind of action to which one is bound)—for it is an external duty in Ethics as well as in justice [15]—but because the legislation in this case is internal and cannot have an external legislator. For the same reason, duties of benevolence, though they are external duties (obligations to external actions), are reckoned as belonging to Ethics because their legislation can only be internal.

To be sure, Ethics also has duties peculiar to itself (for example, duties to oneself); but it also has duties in common with justice, though the manner of being bound to such duties differs. The peculiarity of ethical legislation is that it requires actions to be performed simply because they are duties and makes the basic principles of duty itself, no matter whence the duty arises, into the sufficient incentive of will. Hence, though there are many directly ethical duties, internal legislation also makes all the rest indirectly ethical. 221

IV

RUDIMENTARY CONCEPTS OF THE METAPHYSICS OF MORALS
(*Philosophia practica universalis*)

The concept of freedom is a pure concept of reason. In consequence it is transcendent for theoretical philosophy; that is, it is a concept for which no corresponding example can be given in any possible experience. Accordingly, it does not

[15] [See note 14.]

constitute an object of any theoretical knowledge that is possible for us; and it can by no means be valid as a constitutive principle of speculative reason, but can be valid only as a regulative and, indeed, merely negative principle of speculative reason. In the practical exercise of reason, however, the concept of freedom proves its reality through practical basic principles. As laws of a causality of pure reason, these principles determine the will independently of all empirical conditions (independently of anything sensible) and prove the existence in us of a pure Will in which moral concepts and laws have their origin.

On this concept of freedom, which is positive (from a practical point of view), are founded unconditional practical laws, which are called *moral*. For us, these moral laws are imperatives (commands or prohibitions), for the will is sensibly affected and therefore does not of itself conform to the pure Will, but often opposes it. Moreover, they are categorical (unconditional) imperatives. In being unconditional, they are distinguished from technical imperatives (precepts of skill), which always give only conditional commands. According to these categorical imperatives, certain actions are allowed or not allowed, that is, are morally possible or impossible. However, some actions or their opposites are, according to these imperatives, morally necessary, that is, obligatory. Hence, for such actions there arises the concept of a duty, the obedience to or transgression of which is, to be sure, combined with a pleasure or displeasure of a special kind (that of a moral feeling). But we can take no account of this pleasure or displeasure in the practical laws of reason because these feelings do not relate to the ground of the practical laws, but only to the subjective effect on the mind that accompanies the determination of our will by these laws, and because such feelings can differ greatly in different persons without objectively—that is, in the judgment of reason—adding or taking away anything from the validity or influence of these laws.

222   The following concepts are common to both parts of the metaphysics of morals.

Obligation is the necessity of a free action under a categorical imperative of reason.

An imperative is a practical rule through which an action, in itself contingent, is made necessary. An imperative is distinguished from a practical law by the fact that, though the latter represents the necessity of an action, it does not consider whether this necessity already necessarily resides internally in the acting subject (as in the case of a holy being) or whether it is contingent (as in man). Where the former is the case, there is no imperative. Accordingly, an imperative is a rule the representation of which makes necessary a subjectively contingent action and thus represents the subject as one who must be constrained (necessitated) to conform to this rule.

The categorical (unconditional) imperative is one that does not command mediately, through the representation of an end that could be attained by an action, but immediately, through the mere representation of this action itself (its form), which the categorical imperative thinks as objectively necessary and makes necessary. Examples of this kind of imperative can be supplied by no other practical discipline than the one that prescribes obligation (moral philosophy). All other imperatives are technical and altogether conditional. The ground of the possibility of categorical imperatives lies in the fact that they refer to no determination of will (through which a purpose can be ascribed to it) other than its freedom.

An action is *allowed* (*licitum*) if it is not opposed to obligation, and this freedom that is not limited by any opposing imperative is call competence [16] (*facultas moralis*). Hence it is obvious what is meant by unallowed (*illicitum*).

Duty is that action to which a person is bound. It is therefore the content [*Materie*] of obligation. And there can be one and the same duty (so far as the action is concerned), even though we could be obligated thereto in different ways.

[16] [*Befugnis*—"moral power," "authorization."]

223

The categorical imperative, inasmuch as it asserts an obligation with regard to certain actions, is a morally practical law. But, because obligation includes, not only practical necessity (of the sort that a law in general asserts), but also constraint, the imperative mentioned is a law either of command or of prohibition, according to whether the performance or the nonperformance is represented as a duty. An action that is neither commanded nor prohibited is merely allowed, because with respect to it there is no law that limits freedom (competence) and, therefore, also no duty. Such an action is called morally indifferent (*indifferens, adiaphoron, res merae facultatis*). We may ask whether there are any such actions and, if there are, whether in order to be free to do or forbear as one wants there must be a law of permission (*lex permissiva*) in addition to the laws of command (*lex praeceptiva, lex mandati*) and of prohibition (*lex prohibitiva, lex vetiti*). If so, then competence would not always relate to an indifferent action (*adiaphoron*), for no special law would be required for an indifferent action when it is considered under moral laws.

An action is called a *deed* insofar as it stands under laws of obligation and, consequently, insofar as the subject is considered in this action [or obligation] under the aspect of the freedom of his will. Through such an act, the agent is regarded as the originator of the effect, and this effect together with the action itself can be imputed to him if he is previously acquainted with the law by virtue of which an obligation rests on him.

A *person* is the subject whose actions are susceptible to imputation. Accordingly, moral personality is nothing but the freedom of a rational being under moral laws (whereas psychological personality is merely the capacity to be conscious of the identity of one's self in the various conditions of one's existence). Hence it follows that a person is subject to no laws other than those that he (either alone or at least jointly with others) gives to himself.

A *thing* is something that is not susceptible to imputation. Every object of free will that itself lacks freedom is therefore called a thing (*res corporalis*). [17]

A deed is *right* or *wrong* in general (*rectum aut minus rectum*) insofar as it is in accordance with or opposed to duty (*factum licitum aut illicitum*), no matter what the content or the origin of the duty may be. A deed opposed to duty is called a *transgression* (*reatus*). 224

An unintentional transgression that can be imputed is called mere neglect (*culpa*). An intentional transgression (that is, one accompanied by the consciousness that it is a transgression) is called a crime (*dolus*). That which is right according to external laws is called just (*justum*); what is not so is unjust (*injustum*).

A conflict of duties (*collisio officiorum s. obligationum*) would be that relationship between duties by virtue of which one would (wholly or partially) cancel the other. Because, however, duty and obligation are in general concepts that express the objective practical necessity of certain actions and because two mutually opposing rules cannot be necessary at the same time, then, if it is a duty to act according to one of them, it is not only not a duty but contrary to duty to act according to the other. It follows, therefore, that a conflict of duties and obligations is inconceivable (*obligationes non colliduntur*). It may, however, very well happen that two grounds of obligation (*rationes obligandi*), one or the other of which is inadequate to bind as a duty [*Verpflichtung*] (*rationes obligandi non obligantes*), are conjoined in a subject and in the rule that he prescribes to himself, and then one of the grounds is not a duty. When two such grounds are in conflict, practical philosophy does not say that the stronger obligation prevails (*fortior obligatio vincit*), but that the stronger ground binding to a duty [*Verpflichtungsgrund*] prevails (*fortior obligandi ratio vincit*).[18]

In general, those binding laws for which an external legisla-

---

17 ["Corporeal things"—a concept borrowed from Roman law.]
18 ["The stronger ground of obligation wins."]

tion is possible are called *external laws (leges externae)*. Among external laws, those to which an obligation can be recognized a priori by reason without external legislation are *natural laws*, whereas those that would neither obligate nor be laws without actual external legislation are called *positive laws*. Hence it is possible to conceive of an external legislation which contains only positive laws; but then it would have to be preceded by a natural law providing the ground of the authority of the legislator (that is, his authorization to obligate others through his mere will).

225 A basic principle that makes certain actions a duty is a practical law. The rule that the agent adopts on subjective grounds as his principle is called his *maxim;* hence, the maxims of agents may differ greatly with regard to the same laws.

The categorical imperative, which in general only asserts what obligation is, is this: act according to a maxim that can at the same time be valid as a universal law. You must therefore first of all consider your actions according to their basic subjective principle. But you can recognize whether this basic principle is also objectively valid only by this: that, when your reason puts this principle to the test of conceiving yourself as at the same time universally legislating by means of it, it qualifies for such a universal legislation.

In comparison to the great and manifold consequences [19] that can be drawn from this law, its simplicity must at first seem surprising, as must also its authority to command without appearing to carry any incentive with it. But, in our astonishment at the capacity of our reason to determine will by the mere Idea of the qualification of a maxim for the universality of a practical law, we learn that it is just these practical (moral) laws that first make known a property of will at which speculative reason could never have arrived either from a priori grounds or through experience, and the possibility of which speculative reason could by no means prove even if it did arrive at it, although such practical laws incontestably

---

[19] [*Folgerungen* ("consequences") in First Edition; *Forderungen* ("requirements") in Second Edition.]

prove this property, namely, freedom. Consequently, it should surprise us less to find these laws indemonstrable and yet apodeictic, like mathematical postulates. At the same time, we will see a whole field of practical knowledge open before us, a field that is absolutely closed to reason in its theoretical use when it treats the same Idea of freedom or, indeed, any other of its Ideas of the supersensible.

The agreement of an action with the law of duty is its *legality* (*legalitas*); that of the maxim of the action with the law is its *morality* (*moralitas*). A *maxim* is the subjective principle of action that the subject adopts as a rule for himself (namely, how he wants to act). On the other hand, the basic principle of duty is that which reason absolutely and therefore objectively commands (how he should act).

The supreme basic principle of moral philosophy is therefore: act according to a maxim that can at the same time be valid as a universal law. Every maxim that does not so qualify is opposed to morality [*Moral*]. 226

Laws proceed from the Will; maxims, from the will. In man, the will is free. The Will, which relates to nothing but the law, cannot be called either free or unfree, for it relates, not to actions, but immediately to legislation for the maxims of action (and is therefore practical reason itself). Consequently, it is absolutely necessary and is itself incapable of constraint. Only will can, therefore, be called free.

Freedom of will cannot be defined, however, as the capacity to choose [*Wahl*] to act for or against the law (*libertas indifferentiae*), as some people have tried to define it, even though as a phenomenon it provides frequent examples of this in experience. For freedom (as it first becomes known to us through the moral law) is known only as a negative property within us, the property of not being constrained to action by any sensible determining grounds. As a noumenon, however—that is, according to the capacity of man considered merely as an intelligence—freedom cannot by any means be theoretically described in its positive character as it constrains sensible will. But we can see clearly that, although experience tells us that man as a sensible being exhibits a capacity to choose [*zu wählen*], not only in accordance with the law, but also in opposition to it, yet his freedom as an intelligible being cannot be thus defined, for appearances can never enable us to comprehend a supersensible object (as is free will). Furthermore, we can see that freedom can never be posited on the fact that the rational subject is able to choose in opposition to his (legislative) reason, even though experience proves often enough that this does happen (and yet we cannot comprehend the possibility of this).

It is one thing to admit a proposition (of experience) and quite another to make it both the defining principle (of the concept of free will) and the universal mark distinguishing free will from *arbitrio bruto s. servo* ["brute or servile will"], since in the first case we do not claim that the mark necessarily belongs to the concept, which we are required to do in the latter case. Only the freedom relating to the internal legislation of reason is properly a capacity; the possibility of deviating from it is an incapacity. How, then, can the former be explained by the latter? Such an explanation is a bastard definition (*definitio hybrida*), for it adds to the practical concept the exercise of it as experience teaches it; it presents the concept in a false light.

227

A *law* (a morally practical one) is a proposition that contains a categorical imperative (a command). He who commands (*imperans*) through a law is the *lawgiver* (*legislator*). He is the originator (*auctor*) of the obligation imposed by the law, but is not always the originator of the law. If he is, then the law is positive (contingent) and arbitrary. The law that binds us a priori and unconditionally through our own reason can also be expressed as proceeding from the Will of a supreme lawgiver, that is, of one who has only rights and no duties (accordingly, from the divine Will). But this only signifies the Idea of a moral being whose Will is law for all, yet without conceiving of him as the originator of the law.

Imputation (*imputatio*) in its moral meaning is the judgment by which someone is regarded as the originator (*causa libera* ["free cause"]) of an action, which is then called a "deed" (*factum*) and stands under laws. If this judgment also carries with it the juridical consequences of this deed, it is a judicial [*rechtskräftig*] imputation (*imputatio judiciaria s. valida*); otherwise it is only a criticizing imputation (*imputatio diiudicatoria*). That person (physical or moral) who is authorized to exercise judicial imputation is called the *judge* or the *court* (*judex s. forum*).

What anyone does in accordance with duty beyond what he can be compelled to do by the law is *meritorious* (*meritum*); what he does only in accordance with the law is *debt owed* (*debitum*); finally, what he does that is less than the law demands is *moral demerit* (*demeritum*). The juridical effect of demerit is punishment (*poena*); that of a meritorious deed is reward (*praemium*), provided that the reward promised in the law was the moving cause of the deed. Conduct that agrees with debt owed has no juridical effect. Charitable recompense 228 (*remuneratio s. repensio benefica*) relates to the deed in no way that involves justice [*Rechtsverhältnis*].

The good or bad consequences of an action owed as well as the consequences of omitting a meritorious action cannot be imputed to the subject (*modus imputationis tollens*).

The good consequences of a meritorious action as well as the bad consequences of an illegitimate action can be imputed to the subject (*modus imputationis ponens*).

Subjectively considered, the degree of imputability (*imputabilitas*) of actions must be estimated by the magnitude of the obstacles that have to be overcome. The greater the natural obstacles (of sensibility) and the less the moral obstacle (of duty), the higher is the imputation of merit in a good deed, for example, if, at a considerable sacrifice, I rescue from dire necessity a man who is a complete stranger to me.

On the other hand, the less the natural obstacle and the greater the obstacle from grounds of duty, so much the more is transgression (as demerit) imputed. Therefore, the state of mind of the subject, namely, whether he committed the deed with emotion or in cool deliberation, makes a significant difference in imputation.

THE METAPHYSICS OF MORALS

Part 1

THE METAPHYSICAL
ELEMENTS OF JUSTICE

Introduction

INTRODUCTION TO THE ELEMENTS
OF JUSTICE

§ A. WHAT JURISPRUDENCE IS

The body of those laws that are susceptible of being made into external laws, that is, externally legislated, [constitutes justice and here] is called jurisprudence (*Jus*). Where these laws have actually been externally legislated, the body of them is called positive Law. A specialist in the latter, or a jurist (*Jurisconsultus*), is said to be skilled in the law (*Jurisperitus*) if he knows these external laws also "externally," in the sense that he knows how to apply them to concrete cases presented in experience. Such knowledge can also be called legal knowledge (*Jurisprudentia*). Without the two together, however, it is pure juridical science (*Jurisscientia*). The last designation applies to the systematic knowledge of natural Law (*Jus naturae*), although a specialist in natural Law must provide the immutable principles for all positive legislation.[1]

§ B. WHAT IS JUSTICE?

This question can be just as perplexing for a jurist as the well-known question "What is truth?" is for a logician, assuming, that is, that he does not want to lapse into a mere tautology or to refer us to the laws of a particular country at a par-

---

[1] [The construction of the last three sentences is so ambiguous that it is not clear whether Kant intends the term "juridical science" to apply to the science of positive Law, of natural Law, or of both. But the nomenclature introduced here has little significance for the rest of this treatise. The German terms are as follows:

"jurisprudence"—*Rechtslehre*   "jurist"—*Rechtsgelehrte*
"positive Law"—*positives Recht*   "legally skilled"—*rechtserfahren*
"legal specialist"—*Rechtskundige*   "legal knowledge"—*Rechtsklugheit*
"juridical science"—*Rechtswissenschaft*.]

ticular time. A jurist can, of course, tell us what the actual Law of the land is (*quid sit juris*), that is, what the laws say or have said at a certain time and at a certain place. But whether what these laws prescribe is also just and the universal criterion that will in general enable us to recognize what is just or unjust (*justum et injustum*)—the answer to such questions will remain hidden from him unless, for a while, he abandons empirical principles and searches for the sources of these judgments in pure reason. [To do so is necessary] in order to lay the foundations of any possible positive legislation. (Although [the empirical knowledge of these actual laws] can provide us with helpful clues), a purely empirical theory of justice and Law (like the wooden head in Phaedrus'[2] fable) is very beautiful, but, alas, it has no brain!

230 appears beside "will remain hidden" in margin.

The concept of justice, insofar as it relates to an obligation corresponding to it (that is, the moral concept of justice), applies [only under the following three conditions]. First, it applies only to the external and—what is more—practical relationship of one person to another in which their actions can in fact exert an influence on each other (directly or indirectly). Second, the concept applies only to the relationship of a will to another person's will, not to his wishes or desires (or even just his needs), which are the concern of acts of benevolence and charity. Third, the concept of justice does not take into consideration the matter [content] of the will, that is, the end that a person intends to accomplish by means of the object that he wills; for example, we do not ask whether someone who buys wares from me for his own business will profit from the transaction. Instead, in applying the concept of justice we take into consideration only the form of the relationship between the wills insofar as they are regarded as free, and whether the action of one of them can be conjoined with the freedom of the other in accordance with a universal law.

Justice is therefore the aggregate of those conditions under which the will of one person can be conjoined with the will of another in accordance with a universal law of freedom.

2 [A Roman fabulist of the early first century after Christ.]

§ C. UNIVERSAL PRINCIPLE OF JUSTICE

"Every action is just [right] that in itself or in its maxim is such that the freedom of the will of each can coexist together with the freedom of everyone in accordance with a universal law."

If, therefore, my action or my condition in general can coexist with the freedom of everyone in accordance with a universal law, then anyone who hinders me in performing the action or in maintaining the condition does me an injustice, inasmuch as this hindrance (this opposition) cannot coexist   231 with freedom in accordance with universal laws.

It also follows that I cannot be required to adopt as one of my maxims this principle of all maxims, that is, to make this principle a maxim of my action. For anyone can still be free, even though I am quite indifferent to his freedom or even though I might in my heart wish to infringe on his freedom, as long as I do not through an external action violate his freedom. That I adopt as a maxim the maxim of acting justly is a requirement that Ethics [rather than jurisprudence] imposes on me.

Hence the universal law of justice is: act externally in such a way that the free use of your will is compatible with the freedom of everyone according to a universal law. Admittedly, this law imposes an obligation on me, but I am not at all expected, much less required, to restrict my freedom to these conditions for the sake of this obligation itself. Rather, reason says only that, in its very Idea, freedom is restricted in this way and may be so restricted by others in practice. Moreover, it states this as a postulate not susceptible of further proof. Given that we do not intend to teach virtue, but only to give an account of what is just, we may not and ought not to represent this law of justice as being itself an incentive.

§ D. JUSTICE IS UNITED WITH THE AUTHORIZATION TO USE COERCION

Any opposition that counteracts the hindrance of an effect promotes that effect and is consistent with it. Now, everything that is unjust is a hindrance to freedom according to universal laws. Coercion, however, is a hindrance or opposition to freedom. Consequently, if a certain use of freedom is itself a hindrance to freedom according to universal laws (that is, is unjust), then the use of coercion to counteract it, inasmuch as it is the prevention of a hindrance to freedom, is consistent with freedom according to universal laws; in other words, this use of coercion is just. It follows by the law of contradiction that justice [a right] is united with the authorization to use coercion against anyone who violates justice [or a right].

232   § E. STRICT JUSTICE CAN ALSO BE REPRESENTED
AS THE POSSIBILITY OF A GENERAL RECIPROCAL
USE OF COERCION THAT IS CONSISTENT WITH
THE FREEDOM OF EVERYONE
IN ACCORDANCE WITH
UNIVERSAL LAWS

This statement amounts to saying that justice [or a right] cannot be conceived of as composed of two separate parts, namely, the obligation implied by a law and the authorization that someone has, by virtue of obligating another through his will, to use coercion to make the other fulfill [his obligation]. Instead, the concept of justice [or of a right] can be held to consist immediately of the possibility of the conjunction of universal reciprocal coercion with the freedom of everyone. Just as justice in general has as its object only what is external in actions, so strict justice, inasmuch as it contains no ethical elements, requires no determining grounds of the will besides those that are purely external, for only then is it pure and not confused wtih any prescriptions of virtue. Consequently, strict (narrow) justice is that which alone can be called wholly external. Strict justice is admittedly founded on the consciousness of each person's obligation under the law; but, if it is to remain pure, this consciousness may not and cannot be invoked as an incentive in order to determine the will to act in accordance with it. For this reason, strict justice relies instead on the principle of the possibility of external coercion that is compatible with the freedom of everyone in accordance with universal laws.

Accordingly, when it is said that a creditor has a right to demand from his debtor the payment of a debt, this does not mean that he can persuade the debtor that his own reason itself obligates him to this performance; on the contrary, to say that he has such a right means only that the use of coercion to make anyone do this is entirely compatible with everyone's freedom, including the freedom of the debtor, in accordance with universal laws. Thus "right" [or "justice"] and "authorization to use coercion" mean the same thing.

The law of a reciprocal use of coercion that is necessarily consistent with everyone's freedom under the principle of universal freedom may in certain respects be regarded as the *construction* of this concept [of justice]; that is, it exhibits this concept in a pure a priori intuition on the analogy of the possibility of the free movement of bodies under the law of the equality of action and reaction. Just as in pure mathematics we cannot immediately deduce the properties of the object from a concept, but can only discover them by means of the construction of the concept, so likewise the exhibition and description of the concept of justice is not made possible so much by the concept itself as by the general reciprocal and equal use of coercion that comes under a universal law and is consistent with it. In the same way that this dynamic concept [of the equality of action and reaction] still has a ground in a purely formal concept of pure mathematics (for example, of geometry), reason has also taken as much care as possible to provide the understanding with a priori intuitions to aid in the construction of the concept of justice.[3]

233

3 [This passage is complicated because Kant seems in fact to be calling attention to three distinct analogies. First, there is an analogy between the free movements of human beings and those of bodies, in that the law of the equality of action and reaction, reciprocal coercion, makes "freedom"

[A geometrical analogy may also throw light on the concept of justice and right. In geometry, there are two uses of the term "right" (*rectum*).] On the one hand, we may speak of a right line [straight line], in which case the opposite of "right" is "curved" [or "crooked"]; or on the other hand, we may speak of a right angle, in which case the opposite is "oblique." [4] The unique feature of a right line is that only one such line can be drawn between two points; similarly, where two lines intersect or join each other, there can be only one right angle. The perpendicular forming the right angle may not incline more to one side than to the other, and it divides the space on both sides equally. This bears an analogy to jurisprudence, which wants to know exactly (with mathematical pre-

---

possible in both cases. Another analogy appears in the introduction of the typical Kantian concept of a "construction of a concept." "To *construct* a concept means to exhibit *a priori* the intuition which corresponds to a concept. . . . Thus I construct a triangle by representing the object which corresponds to this concept either by imagination alone, in pure intuition, or in accordance therewith also on paper, in empirical intuition—in both cases completely *a priori*, without having borrowed the pattern from any experience. The single figure which we draw is empirical, and yet it serves to express the concept, without impairing its universality"—*Critique of Pure Reason*, trans. Kemp Smith, B 741–742. According to Kant, all mathematical knowledge is gained from the construction of concepts. In other words, in order to accomplish a complete analysis of the concept of justice, we need to resort to more concrete phenomena (for example, the use of coercion). Finally, at the end of this passage, Kant introduces a third analogy which points up the necessity for having "intermediate" concepts; thus, geometry provides "intermediate concepts" for physics, and similarly there must be "intermediate concepts" in Law.]

[4] [The translation into English of the next few lines is rendered difficult because of the various uses of the German word *Recht*. I have consequently translated rather freely, without, however, fundamentally changing the sense of the original. It may be pointed out that Kant was without doubt deliberately making puns in this passage, because he goes out of his way to use certain expressions. Thus, besides punning on *Recht*, he was punning on *krumm* ("curved"), which also means "crooked" or "dishonest," and on *schief* ("oblique"), which may mean "askew" or "crooked."]

cision) what the property of everyone is. In ethics, in contrast, such narrow exactitude should not be expected, since it cannot refuse to make some room for exceptions (*latitudinem*).

But, without having to enter the field of Ethics, we are confronted with two cases that claim to be decidable by justice, but for which no one can be found who could decide them and which, as it were, belong to Epicurus' *intermundia* ["spaces between the worlds"]. These two cases must first be excluded from jurisprudence proper, to which we shall presently proceed, so that their shaky principles will not acquire any influence on the fixed basic principles of that discipline itself.

Appendix to the Introduction to the Elements of Justice

Equivocal Rights (*Jus aequivocum*)

All justice and every right in the narrower sense (*jus strictum*) are united with the authorization to use coercion. But one can also think of justice or rights in a wider sense (*jus latum*), where the authorization to use coercion cannot be stipulated by any law. Now, there are two true or supposed rights of this kind—equity and the right of necessity. The first admits a right without any coercion; the second, coercion without any right. It can be easily seen that this equivocation arises from the fact that there are cases in which a right with regard to which no judge could be appointed to render a decision is called into question.

I

Equity (*Aequitas*)

When one appeals to equity (regarded objectively) as the ground of a demand, he is by no means basing this demand solely on the ethical duties of others (their benevolence and kindness); on the contrary, he is basing it on his right. In the case of a right of equity, however, the requisite conditions according to which the judge is able to stipulate how much or what kind of remedy should be allowed for the claim in question are absent. [For example,] when one of the partners of a mercantile company formed under the condition of sharing the profits equally has nevertheless done more for the company than the other members and through various mishaps has thereby lost more than the others, then on the grounds of equity he can demand that he receive more than an equal share. If he rests his case solely on justice proper (strict Law), his request will be refused, because—if one imagines a judge in his case—the judge has no definite particulars (data) to serve as a guide in rendering a decision as to how much he should receive according to the contract. Again, a domestic servant whose wages through the end of the year have been paid in a currency that has in the intervening period become depreciated, with the result that he can no longer buy what he could have bought with the same money at the time of concluding the contract, cannot appeal to a right to be compensated for the loss caused by the fact that the same amount of money no longer has the same value. He can only appeal to equity (a silent goddess who cannot be heard), because nothing was stipulated about this in the contract, and a judge cannot pronounce in accordance with unstipulated conditions.

From this it follows that a court of equity (for disputes with others over their rights) contains a self-contradiction. Only when the rights of the judge himself are involved and over 235 matters of which he can dispose for his own person may and should there be any hearing for equity. For example, this might happen in a case in which the Crown itself takes over the loss that others have suffered in its service and for which remedy is requested, although by strict justice it has a strict right to reject the claim on the grounds that they undertook the service at their own risk.

Indeed, the motto (*dictum*) of equity is: "The strictest justice is the greatest injustice" (*summum jus summa injuria*); there is, however, no remedy for this evil in actual legal proceedings, even though a claim of justice is involved. The claim belongs solely to the court of conscience (*forum poli*), whereas every question regarding the actual Law of the land must be taken before a civil court (*forum soli*).[5]

II
The Right of Necessity (*Jus necessitatis*)

This imagined right is supposed to give me permission to take the life of another person when my own life is in danger, even if he has done me no harm. It is quite obvious that this conception implies a self-contradiction within jurisprudence, since the point in question here has nothing to do with an unjust assailant on my own life, which I defend by taking his life (*jus inculpatae tutelae*), for even in such a situation the recommendation of moderation (*moderamen*) is not part of justice, but belongs only to Ethics. The question under discussion is whether I am permitted to use violence against someone who himself has not used it against me.

It is clear that this allegation [of a right based on necessity] is not to be understood objectively, according to what a law might prescribe, but merely subjectively, as the sentence might be pronounced in a court of law. There could be no penal law assigning the death penalty to a man who has been shipwrecked and finds himself struggling with another man—both in equal danger of losing their lives—and who, in order to save his own life, pushes the other man off the plank on which he had saved himself. For the first man, no punishment threatened by the law could be greater than losing his life. A penal law applying to such a situation could never have the effect intended, for the threat of an evil that is still uncertain (being condemned to death by a judge) cannot outweigh the fear of an evil that is certain (being drowned). Hence, we must judge that, although an act of self-preservation through 236 violence is not inculpable (*inculpabile*) [*unsträflich*], it still is unpunishable (*impunibilie*) [*unstrafbar*], and this subjective immunity from punishment, through a strange confusion

5 [*Das Gewissensgericht; das bürgerliche Recht. Forum poli* means "the court of heaven" (*polus* = "heaven"), and *forum soli* means "the court of the earth" (*solum* = "earth").]

among jurists, is identified with an objective (legal) immunity from punishment.

The motto of the right of necessity is: "Necessity has no law" (*necessitas non habet legem*); but there still cannot be any necessity that will make what is unjust legal.

It is apparent that, in both kinds of judgment concerning justice and rights (equity and the right of necessity), the equivocation arises from a confusion of the objective with the subjective grounds of the exercise of justice (before reason and before a court). Thus, on the one hand, what one himself recognizes on good grounds to be just will not receive confirmation in a court of justice, and, on the other hand, what he must judge unjust in itself will be treated with indulgence by the court. This is a consequence of the fact that the term "justice" [or "right"] is not used with the same meaning in the two cases.

DIVISION OF THE THEORY OF JUSTICE

A. GENERAL DIVISION OF THE DUTIES OF JUSTICE

In this division, we can well use Ulpian's [6] formulas provided that we give them a meaning that he himself indeed may not have had in mind but that can still be developed from them or given to them.

(1) *Be an honorable man* (*honeste vive*). Juridical honor consists in asserting one's own worth as a human being in relation to others, and this duty is expressed in the proposition: "Do not make yourself into a mere means for others, but be at the same time an end for them." This duty will be explained later [7] as an obligation resulting from the right of humanity in our own person (*lex justi*).

(2) *Do no one an injustice* (*neminem laede*), even if on this

---

[6] [Domitius Ulpianus, Roman jurist (*fl.* A.D. 211–228). About one-third of Justinian's *Digest* consists of selections from Ulpian. These famous three general precepts are to be found in Justinian's *Institutes* I. 1. 3.]

[7] [Kant is probably referring to *The Metaphysical Elements of Virtue*, § 11.]

account you should have to stop associating with others and to avoid society altogether (*lex juridica*).

(3) (If you cannot avoid the latter [i.e., society]), enter into 237 a society with others in which each person can get and keep what is his own (*suum cuique tribue*). If the original formula is translated literally as "give to each what is his own," it would be nonsense, inasmuch as one cannot give to someone something that he already has. In order to make sense of this formula, it must be interpreted to mean: "Enter into a condition under which what is his own is guaranteed to each person against everyone else" (*lex justitiae*).

Thus, these three classical formulas serve at the same time as principles of the division of the system of duties of justice into internal, external, and those that contain the derivation of the latter from the former through subsumption.[8]

B. GENERAL DIVISION OF JUSTICE

(1) [Justice in the sense of Law.] Law considered as a system [of laws] [*systematische Lehren*] can be divided into natural Law, which rests on nothing but a priori principles, and positive (statutory) Law, which proceeds from the Will of a legislator.

(2) [Justice in the sense in which it refers to rights.] Rights, considered as (moral) capacities [*moralische Vermögen*] to bind others, provide the lawful ground for binding others (*titulum*). The main division of rights is into innate rights and acquired rights. An innate right is one that belongs to everyone by nature, independently of any juridical act; an acquired right requires such an act.

Innate property can also be called internal property (*meum vel tuum internum*), for what is external must always be acquired.

There Is Only One Innate Right
Freedom (independence from the constraint of another's

---

8 [Kant appears to be saying that the external duty not to injure others can be derived from the internal duty to assert one's own rights by using the duty to enter into civil society as an intermediary premise.]

will), insofar as it is compatible with the freedom of everyone else in accordance with a universal law, is the one sole and original right that belongs to every human being by virtue of his humanity.

[This principle of innate freedom contains within itself all the following rights:] Innate equality, that is, independence from being bound by others to do more than one can also reciprocally bind them to do; hence also the attribute of a human being's being his own master (*sui juris*) and of being an irreproachable man (*justi*), inasmuch as, prior to any juridical act, he has done no injustice to anyone; finally, also the authorization [or liberty] to do anything to others that does not by itself detract from what is theirs and that would not detract if only they themselves were not willing to submit themselves to it; an example of this would be merely sharing one's thoughts with others or telling or promising them something, no matter whether what is said is true and honest or false and dishonest (*veriloquium aut falsiloquium*), for it is entirely up to them whether they want to believe him.[9] All these authorizations are already contained in the principle of innate freedom and are really not (as species in a division under a higher concept of right) distinct from it.

The purpose of introducing this further division of the system of natural Law with respect to innate rights was that, when a controversy arises over an acquired right and the ques-

---

[9] Indeed, the deliberate telling of a falsehood, even if it is done in a frivolous manner, is ordinarily called a lie (*mendacium*), because at the very least it can harm him who, after faithfully repeating the lie to others, thereby becomes a laughingstock on account of his gullibility. In the juridical sense, however, a falsehood is called a lie only if it is immediately prejudicial to the right of another; such as, for example, the false allegation that a contract has been concluded with someone in order to deprive him of what is his (*falsiloquium dolosum*). This distinction between closely related concepts is not ungrounded, because, when a person simply states his thoughts, the other always remains free to accept them as he pleases. Nevertheless, the well-founded rumor that such a person is one whose talk cannot be believed comes so close to calling him a liar that here the borderline that separates what belongs to *jus* [justice] from what belongs to Ethics is scarcely discernible.

tion is raised as to who has the burden of proof *(onus probandi)* —either with respect to a disputed fact or, if this is settled, with respect to a disputed right—someone who denies this obligation [to prove his case] can methodically appeal to his innate right of freedom (which can now be specified according to his various relations) as though he were invoking various titles of right.

Since with regard to innate, internal property there are not [several] rights, but only one, the two parts that make up this superior division are utterly unequal and dissimilar. Hence it can be put among the prolegomena, the preliminary observations; and the division of the elements of justice [jurisprudence] will be concerned with external property only.

DIVISION OF THE METAPHYSICS OF MORALS IN GENERAL

239

I

All duties are either duties of justice *(officia juris)*, that is, those for which external legislation is possible, or duties of virtue *(officia virtutis s. ethica)*, for which such legislation is not possible. The latter cannot be the subject matter of external legislation because they refer to an end that is (or the adoption of which is) at the same time a duty, and no external legislation can effect the adoption of an end (because that is an internal act of the mind), although external actions might be commanded that would lead to this [end], without the subject himself making them his end.

Inasmuch as duties and rights are related to each other, why is moral *(Moral)* philosophy usually (for example, by Cicero) labeled the theory of duties and not also of rights? The reason for this is that we know our own freedom (from which all moral laws and hence all rights as well as duties are derived) only through the moral imperative, which is a proposition commanding duties; the capacity to obligate others to a duty, that is, the concept of a right, can be subsequently derived from this imperative.

II

In the theory of duties, man can and should be represented from the point of view of the property of his capacity for freedom, which is completely supersensible, and so simply from the point of view of his humanity considered as a personality, independently of physical determinations (*homo noumenon*). In contradistinction to this, man can be regarded as a subject affected by these determinations (*homo phaenomenon*). Accordingly, [the ideas of] right and end, which are related to duty under these two aspects, will in turn give us the following division.

240   **Division According to the Objective Relationship of the Law to Duty**

Perfect duty

1. The right of humanity in our own person	of justice Duty of virtue	**2.** The right of men
3. The end of humanity in our own person		**4.** The end of men

Duty to oneself (left side)   *Duty to others* (right side)

Imperfect duty

III

241   Inasmuch as subjects may be related to one another in several ways with respect to the relationship of right to duty (genuinely or spuriously), a division can also be made from this point of view.

Division According to the Subjective Relationship Between the Subject Who Imposes the Duty and the Subject Bound by the Duty

1.

The juridical relationship of man to beings who have neither rights nor duties.

Vacat,[10] since these are non-rational beings who do not bind us, nor could we be bound by them.

2.

The juridical relationship of man to beings who have both rights and duties.

Adest,[11] since this is a relationship of men to men.

3.

The juridical relationship of man to beings who have only duties but no rights.

Vacat, since these would be beings without personality (serfs, slaves).

4.

The juridical relationship of man to a being who has only rights but no duties (God).

Vacat; that is, in pure philosophy, because it is not an object of possible experience.

Thus a real relationship between right and duty can occur only under Number Two. The reason that such a relationship is not to be found under Number Four is that it would require a transcendent duty, that is, a duty for which no external subject imposing the duty can be given. Hence, the relationship is only ideal from the theoretical point of view; that is, it is a relationship to an object of thought that we make for ourselves, although the concept thereof is not completely empty, but one that is fruitful from an internal, practical point of view in relation to ourselves and to maxims of internal morality, inasmuch as our whole immanent (accomplishable) duty consists of this purely imagined relationship. 242

10 [*Vacat* = "has no members."]
11 [*Adest* = "has members."]

Division of Morality as a System of Duties in General

Elements   Methodology

Duties of justice   Duties of virtue   Didactics   Ascetics

Private Law   Public Law   [Moral instruction]   [Moral training]

and so on, everything

that comprises, not only the matter [content], but also the
architectonic form of a systematic moral philosophy [*wissen-
schaftliche Sittenlehre*] until the metaphysical elements will
have laid completely bare the universal principles.[12]

The supreme division of the Law of nature should be, not
into natural and social Law (as it is sometimes thought to be),
but into natural and civil Law. The first of these is called
private Law; the second, public Law. The state of nature is
not opposed and contrasted to the state of society, but to the
civil society, for within a state of nature there can indeed be
a society, but there can be no civil society (that guarantees
property through public law). Therefore, Law in the state
of nature is called private Law.[13]

12 [See Preface, pp. 3–4, for an explanation of what Kant means by
metaphysical elements (*Anfangsgründe*).]

13 [For the distinction between private and public law, see Translator's
Introduction, p. xii.]

I

PRIVATE LAW

I

PRIVATE LAW

§ 1.

An object is mine *de jure* (*meum juris*) if I am so bound to it that anyone else who uses it without my consent thereby injures me. The subjective condition of the possibility of the use of an object is [called] *possession*.

An external thing is mine, however, only if I can assume that it is still possible for me to be injured by someone else's use of the thing even when it is not in my possession. Consepossession means the purely *de jure* possession of the same object.

The expression, "an object is external to me," may mean either that it is simply an object that is different and distinct from me (as subject) or that, in addition to this, the object is in another position (*positus*) in space or time. Only if we take quently, there would be a self-contradiction in the concept of possession if it did not have two meanings, namely, *sensible* possession and *intelligible* possession. Sensible possession means the physical possession of an object, whereas intelligible "external" in the first sense can possession be thought of as rational possession; in the second sense, it would have to be called empirical possession.

246   An *intelligible* possession (if such is possible) is possession without detention (*detentio*).[1]

§ 2. THE JURIDICAL POSTULATE OF PRACTICAL REASON [2]

[This postulate asserts that:] it is possible to have any and every external object of my will as my property. In other words, a maxim according to which, if it were made into a law, an object of will would have to be in itself (objectively) ownerless [*herrenlos*] (*res nullius*) [3] conflicts with Law and justice.

[The reason for this postulate is as follows.]

An object of my will is a thing that I have the physical power to use. Let us suppose that it were absolutely not within my power *de jure* to make use of this thing, that is, that such power would not be consistent with the freedom of everyone in accordance with a universal law. In that case, freedom would be robbing itself of the use of its will in relation to an object of the same will inasmuch as it would be placing usable objects outside all possibility of being used. In other words, it would reduce these objects to nought from a practical point of view and make them into *res nullius,* although formally the will involved in the use of these things is still consistent with the freedom of everyone in accordance with universal laws.

Now, pure practical reason provides as a basis for the use of the will nothing but formal laws and thus abstracts from the material content of the will, that is, from the remaining characteristics of its object, considering the object only insofar as it is an object of the will. Hence, pure practical reason can

1 [That is, physical custody or control. See Translator's Introduction, pp. xxii–xxiii.]

2 ["By a postulate of pure practical reason, I understand a theoretical proposition which is not as such demonstrable, but which is an inseparable corollary of an a priori unconditionally valid practical law"—*Critique of Practical Reason,* trans. L. W. Beck, "The Library of Liberal Arts," No. 52 (New York: The Liberal Arts Press, 1956), p. 127.]

3 [*Res nullius,* "the property of nobody." Although this is an accepted concept in traditional Roman law, Kant contends that it is an absurdity.]

contain no absolute prohibition concerning the use of an object of this type [*res nullius*], inasmuch as to do so would constitute a contradiction of external freedom with itself.

An object of my will, however, is something of which I have the physical capacity to make use, a use that is within my power (*potentia*). This capacity must be distinguished from having the same object within my authority (*in potestatem meam redactum*).[4] The latter presupposes, not merely a capacity, but also an act of the will. But in order merely to conceive of something as an object of my will, it is sufficient that I be aware of the fact that it is within my [physical] power. Consequently, it is an a priori assumption of practical reason that any and every object of my will be viewed and treated as something that has the objective possibility of being yours or mine.[5]

This postulate can be called a permissive law of practical   247
reason (*lex permissiva*). It confers on us an authorization that we cannot derive from mere concepts of justice in general, namely, the authorization to impose an obligation on all others—an obligation that they otherwise would not have had —to refrain from using certain objects of our will because we were the first to take possession of them. Reason requires that this postulate be taken as a basic principle, and it does this as practical reason extending itself a priori by means of this postulate.

§ 3

He who intends to assert that he holds a thing as his property must be in possession of the object, for, if he were not in possession of the object, then he could not be injured by someone else's using it without his consent. If something that is external to him, but not bound to him *de jure,* affects this object, that something would not be able to affect him himself (the subject) and to wrong him.

4 ["Brought under my authority."]
5 [That is, someone's property.]

§ 4. EXPOSITION OF THE CONCEPT OF EXTERNAL PROPRIETARY RIGHTS BELONGING TO YOU AND ME

Only three kinds of thing can be external objects of my will: (1) a (corporeal) thing external to me; (2) the will of another with respect to a particular act (*praestatio*);[6] (3) the status of another in relation to me. These correspond to the categories of substance, causality, and community between external objects and me in accordance with the laws of freedom.

(a) I cannot call an object in space (a corporeal thing) mine unless I can claim still another actual (nonphysical) kind of possession of that object even when I do not have physical possession of it.

Thus, for example, I do not call an apple mine simply because I hold it in my hand (possess it physically), but only if I can say: "I possess it even when I let it out of the hand that is holding it." Similarly, I cannot say of the land on which I am camping that it is mine just because I am camping on it; I can say that it is mine only if I can assert that it is in my possession even if I leave the place in question. The reason for this is that, in the first case (of empirical possession), if someone were to wrench the apple out of my hand or to carry me off from the place where I was camping, he would not injure me with respect to my external property, although, of course, he would injure what is internally mine (my freedom). But he would not injure me as far as my external property is concerned unless I could also claim to have possession of the object even without detention of it; therefore, in the present case, I cannot call these objects (the apple and the camp) mine.

(b) I cannot call the performance of something through the will of another person mine if I can say only that the performance has come into my possession at the same time as his promise (*pactum re initum*).[7] I can call it mine only if I can

---

[6] [In Roman law, obligations of a personal character, for example, the performance of something promised.]

[7] ["A pact begun through the thing pacted."]

maintain that I would have possession of the will of another (to determine it to this performance) even if the time of the performance is yet to come. The promise of the latter accordingly belongs among my possessions [*Habe und Gut*] (*obligatio activa*), and I can include it under what is mine. But I can count it as belonging to me not merely when I have in my possession what is promised (that is, the first case) but also when I do not yet possess what is promised. Consequently, I must be able to think of myself as having possession of this object [the performance] quite independently of temporal limitations and empirical possession.

(c) I cannot call a wife, a child, a servant, or any other person mine just because I am at present able to command them as members of my household or because I have them under my coercive power and under my authority and in my possession. I can do so only if I can still say that I possess them through my mere Will as long as they are alive in some place and at some time—in other words, if I possess them *de jure*. They belong to my possessions only when and insofar as I can claim the latter.

§ 5. DEFINITION OF THE CONCEPT OF EXTERNAL PROPRIETARY RIGHTS BELONGING TO YOU AND ME

A nominal definition serves only to distinguish the objects defined from all others and precedes the complete and determinate exposition of a concept. The nominal definition of what is externally mine [that is, my property] would be as follows: A thing is externally mine if it is something outside me which is such that any interference with my using it as I please would constitute an injury to me (a violation of my 249 freedom, a freedom that can coexist with the freedom of everyone in accordance with a universal law).

The real definition of this concept, however, suffices for the Deduction of the concept (that is, of the knowledge of the possibility of the object). It is as follows: A thing is externally mine if it is such that any prevention of my use of it would constitute an injury to me even if it is not in my possession (that is, I am not the holder of the object). Nevertheless, I must have some kind of possession of an external object if that object is to be called mine; otherwise, anyone acting against my will so as to affect the object would not at the same time affect me and so also would not injure me. Consequently, following § 4, if there is to be anything externally yours or mine [that is, any property], we must assume that intelligible possession (*possessio noumenon*) is possible. Thus, empirical possession is only possession in appearance (*possessio phae-nomenon*), although in this connection the object that I possess is not regarded as an appearance, as it was in the transcendental analytic [of the *Critique of Pure Reason*], but as a thing-in-itself. That work was concerned with reason as it relates to the theoretical knowledge of the nature of things and with how far it extends. Here, on the other hand, we are concerned with reason as it relates to the practical determination of the will in accordance with laws of freedom, and its object may be known either through the senses or merely through pure reason. Justice [or right] is an example of the latter, for it is a pure, practical, rational concept of the will under laws of freedom.

For this reason, one should not carelessly speak of possessing a right to this or that object. Rather, one should speak of possessing the object rightfully [that is, of possessing it *de jure*]. A right is already an intellectual possession of an object, and "to possess a possession" would be an expression without meaning.

§ 6. DEDUCTION OF THE CONCEPT OF PURELY *DE JURE* POSSESSION OF AN EXTERNAL OBJECT (*Possessio noumenon*)

The question of how it is possible for something to be externally yours or mine [that is, one's property] is now transformed into the question: How is purely *de jure* (intelligible) possession possible? And this question in turn becomes: How is a synthetic a priori proposition concerning rights [*Rechtsatz*] possible?

All propositions about rights are a priori, for they are laws of reason (*dictamina rationis*). A proposition about rights [or justice] with respect to empirical possession is analytic, for it says no more than follows from the concept of empirical possession by the law of contradiction, namely, that, if I am the holder of a thing (that is, physically connected to it), then anyone who touches it without my consent (for example, wrests an apple from my hand) affects and diminishes that which is internally mine (my freedom). Consequently, the maxim of his action stands in direct contradiction to the axiom of justice [rights]. Thus, the proposition concerning empirical possession does not extend beyond the right of a person with respect to himself.

In contrast, the proposition concerning the possibility of possessing a thing outside myself after abstracting from all the conditions of empirical possession in space and time (in other words, the assumption of the possibility of *possessio noumenon*)—this proposition does extend beyond the aforementioned conditions. It is a synthetic proposition, for it postulates as necessary to the concept of what is externally yours or mine [property] a kind of possession not involving detention. Now, it is the task of reason to show how such a proposition that extends beyond the concept of empirical possession is a priori possible.

In this way, taking possession of a secluded piece of land is an act of private will without being an arbitrary usurpation. The possessor bases his act on [the concept of] the innate common possession of the earth's surface and on the a priori general Will corresponding to it, which permits private possession of land (since otherwise unoccupied things [e.g. land] would in themselves and in accordance with a law become ownerless things). Thus, the possessor originally acquires a piece of land through first possession and withstands by right [*mit Recht*] (*jure*) anyone else who might interfere with his private use of it. In a state of nature, however, he cannot do

250

this through legal proceedings [*rechtswegen*] *(de jure),* for there is no public law in that state.

Even if a piece of land is regarded as free or declared to be so, that is, open for everyone's use, one still cannot say that it is free by nature or free originally, prior to any juridical act. Even that would be a relationship to things, namely, to the land that refuses possession of itself to everyone. But this freedom of the land consists in a prohibition addressed to everyone not to help himself to it; for this common possession of the land would be required and cannot take place without a contract.[8] Because a piece of land can be made free only through a contract, it must actually be in the possession of all those (united together) who mutually prohibit to themselves the use thereof or suspend such use.

251   The original community of the land and, along with the land, of the things on it *(communio fundi originaria)* is an Idea that has objective (juridical-practical) reality. This kind of community must be sharply distinguished from the primitive community *(communio primaeva),* which is a fiction. Such a primitive community would have to have been a community founded on and issuing out of a contract, a contract through which everyone is supposed to have renounced his private possessions and to have transformed them into a common possession by uniting the possessions of each with those of everyone else; history would have to provide us with a proof that this happened. To regard such a procedure as an original taking of possession and to hold that the particular possession of each man can and should be grounded on it is a contradiction.

Possession *(possessio)* must also be distinguished from squatting [*Sitz*] *(sedes),* and taking possession of land with the intention of acquiring it must be distinguished from settling or colonizing [*Niederlassung, Ansiedelung*] *(in-*

8 [Following Natorp and Cassirer, this passage is interpreted as saying that the land is free only by virtue of a contract among everyone.]

colatus). The latter is merely the continuing private possession of a place that depends on the presence of the
subject at that place. I am not speaking of settling considered as a second juridical act that can, but need not,
follow taking possession; this kind of settling would not
be an original possession, but one derived from the consent of others.

Purely physical possession (detention) of land already
constitutes a right in a thing, although it is obviously
not sufficient for considering the land mine. In relation to
others, this possession is (as far as one knows) a first possession and as such is consistent with the law of external
freedom and is, at the same time, implied in the original
community of possession, which, in turn, implies the a
priori ground of the possibility of private possession. It
follows that interference with the first holder of a piece
of land in his use of it constitutes an injury. Thus, first
possession has for itself a ground in right [*Rechtsgrund*]
(*titulus possessionis*), and this ground is original common
possession. Hence the proposition, "happy is he who is
in possession" (*beati possidentes*), is a basic principle of
natural justice, for no one is bound to authenticate his
possession. This basic principle sets up the first taking of
possession as a *de jure* ground of acquisition on which
every first possessor can rely.

A *theoretical* a priori basic principle (according to the
Critique of Pure Reason) must have an a priori intuition
underlying the given concept and so [if this principle of
possession were merely theoretical] something else would
have to be added to the concept of the possession of the
object. But, with a *practical* principle [such as this one],
we proceed in the opposite fashion and must remove (abstract from) all the conditions of intuition that provide
the grounds of empirical possession in order to extend the
concept of possession beyond the empirical concept thereof
and be able to say: "Any and every external object that
I have under my authority (and insofar as it is under

252

my authority) can be counted as *de jure* mine without my having to possess it [empirically]."

The possibility of this [nonempirical] kind of possession and the Deduction of the concept of nonempirical possession are founded on the juridical postulate of practical reason: "It is a duty of justice to act toward others so that external objects (usable objects) can also become someone's [property]." The possibility and the Deduction [of nonempirical possession] are at the same time bound up with the exposition of the latter concept [of property], which grounds external property on nonphysical possession alone. The possibility of nonphysical possession cannot in any way be proved by itself, nor can it be immediately intuited as true (simply because it is a concept of reason for which no corresponding intuition can be given). Instead, its possibility follows directly from the aforementioned postulate, for, if it is necessary to act according to this basic principle of right and justice, then the intelligible condition (of a mere *de jure* possession) must also be possible.

It should surprise no one that the *theoretical* principles of external property become lost in the intelligible world and represent no advance in knowledge, for the possibility of the concept of freedom, on which they rest, is not susceptible of theoretical Deduction and can only be deduced from the practical law of reason (the categorical imperative) as a fact [*Faktum*] of practical reason.[9]

§ 7. APPLICATION OF THE PRINCIPLE OF THE POSSIBILITY OF EXTERNAL PROPERTY TO OBJECTS OF EXPERIENCE

The concept of purely *de jure* possession is not an empirical concept (one dependent on temporal and spatial conditions). Nevertheless, it has practical reality; that is, it must be

253

9 [For elaboration of the concept of a fact of practical reason, see *Critique of Practical Reason*, trans. Beck, p. 43.]

applicable to objects of experience, the knowledge of which depends on temporal and spatial conditions.

The procedure with the concept of right [or justice] in relation to the latter [objects of experience] considered as possible external property is as follows: the concept of right, which resides only in reason, cannot be applied directly to objects of experience or to the concept of empirical possession. Instead, it must first be applied to the pure concept of possession in general, which is a pure concept of the understanding. Therefore, instead [of using the concept] of detention (*detentio*), that is, an empirical representation of possession, we must [use] the concept of "having" [*Haben*], abstracted from all spatial and temporal conditions, and think of the object simply as subject to my authority (*in potestate mea positum esse*).[10] For [in this conception of "having"] the expression "external object" does not refer to its existing at a place different from mine nor to the fact that [in a contract] the decision of my Will and my acceptance of an offer take place at a time other than that of the making of the offer; [11] rather, "external" means simply that the object is distinct and different from me. Now, through its law of right [and justice], practical reason requires that, in applying [the concept of] your or my property to objects, we not think of [the concept] in terms of sensible conditions, but in abstraction from them, because we are concerned with the determination of the will in accordance with laws of freedom. This law also requires that we think of the possession of the object [as a concept of the understanding], inasmuch as only a concept of the understanding can be subsumed under concepts of right [and justice]. Thus I can say: I possess a field even though it is located at a place completely different from the one in which I now actually find myself. For we are concerned here only with an intellectual relationship to the object, namely, so far as it is subject to my authority (the concept of posses-

---

10 ["Being placed under my authority."]

11 [Kant refers to the notion of a contract as a meeting of wills.]

sion as a concept of the understanding, which is independent of spatial determinations); and it is mine [my property] because my Will to use the object as I please does not conflict with the law of external freedom.

The ground of the validity of this concept of [*de jure*] possession (*possessio noumenon*) considered as [a concept of] universally valid legislation lies precisely in the fact that practical reason requires that we conceive of the possession of this object of my will quite apart from possession in appearance (detention) and in accordance with concepts of the understanding. That is, it requires that we conceive this kind of possession, not in empirical terms, but in terms of the a priori conditions contained in this concept of the understanding [that is, "having"]. This universally valid legislation is contained in the expression: "This external object is mine." Through this, an obligation is imposed on everyone else to refrain from using the object, an obligation that one would not otherwise have had.

254 Therefore, the relation of having something external to oneself as one's own [property] consists of a purely *de jure* union of the Will of the subject with that object, independently of his relationship to it in space and time and in accordance with the concept of intelligible possession.

A spot on the earth is not externally mine simply because I bodily occupy it (for here only my external freedom—the possession of myself and not the possession of anything outside me—is involved; hence it involves only an internal right). My external right is involved only if, although I have left the place and gone elsewhere, I still possess it. If one wishes to make my continuous and personal occupation of a place into a condition of having it as my property, then either he must maintain that it is not possible to have something external as one's property (which is incompatible with Postulate § 2) or, in order to make this possible, he must demand that I be in two places at the same time; this last, however, is self-contradictory, since it amounts to saying that I should be and should not be at one place.

The same considerations apply to the case in which I have accepted a promise. When I accept a promise, my having [*Habe*] and possession of what is promised is not voided by the fact that at one time the promiser says, "This thing shall be yours," but at a later time says concerning the same thing, "I will now that the thing shall not be yours." The character of such intellectual relationships is such that it is as though he had said without any intervening time between the two declarations of his Will, "It shall be yours, and, also, it shall not be yours," and this contradicts itself.

Again, the same thing holds for the concept of the *de jure* possession of a person so far as he belongs [*zu der Habe gehörend*] to the subject (for example, his wife, child, servant), for a domestic community and the reciprocal possession of the status of all its members are not voided by the liberty [*Befugnis*] they have to be away from one another and in different places. These persons are joined by a *de jure* relationship, and what is externally yours or mine here, as in the previous cases, rests entirely on the assumption of the possibility of a pure rational possession without detention.

In connection with the concept of what is externally yours or mine [that is, external property] juridical-practical reason is actually forced into a critique of itself by an antinomy of propositions concerning the possibility of this kind of possession. Only as a result of an unavoidable dialectic in which the thesis and antithesis make equal claims for the validity of two mutually incompatible sets of conditions is reason, even in its practical employment (involving rights), obliged to distinguish between possession as appearance and possession as conceivable merely through the understanding.

255

The *thesis* states: It is possible to have something external as mine even though I do not have possession of it.

The *antithesis* states: It is not possible to have something external as mine if I do not have possession of it.

Solution: Both propositions are true—the first, when I take the word "possession" to mean empirical possession (*possessio phaenomenon*); the second, when I take it to mean pure intelligible possession (*possessio noumenon*).

The possibility of intelligible possession and hence also of what is externally yours or mine cannot be intuited, but must be inferred from the postulate of practical reason. There is something especially noteworthy in that here practical reason proceeds without intuitions, not needing even a single a priori intuition, and extends itself by simply omitting empirical conditions, a procedure justified by the law of freedom. Thus it can set up synthetic a priori propositions concerning rights [*Rechtssätze*], the proof of which (as will be shown presently) can afterward be carried out in an analytical fashion from a practical point of view.

§ 8. HAVING EXTERNAL THINGS AS ONE'S PROPERTY IS POSSIBLE ONLY IN A JURIDICAL CONDITION OF SOCIETY, UNDER A PUBLIC-LEGISLATIVE AUTHORITY, THAT IS, A CIVIL SOCIETY

When I declare (by word or deed), "I will that an external thing shall be mine," I thereby declare it obligatory for everyone else to refrain from [using] the object of my will. This is an obligation that no one would have apart from this juridical act of mine. Included in this claim, however, is an acknowledgment of being reciprocally bound to everyone else to [exercise] a similar and equal restraint with respect to what is theirs. The obligation involved here comes from a universal rule of the external juridical relationship [that is, the civil society]. Consequently, I am not bound to leave what is another's [property] untouched if everyone else does not in turn guarantee to me with regard to what is mine that he will act in accordance with exactly the same principle. This guarantee does not require a special juridical act, but is already contained in the concept of being externally juridically bound to a duty [*Verpflichtung*] on account of the universality, and

256

hence also the reciprocity, of an obligation coming from a universal rule.

Now, with respect to an external and contingent possession, a unilateral Will cannot serve as a coercive law for everyone, since that would be a violation of freedom in accordance with universal laws. Therefore, only a Will binding everyone else— that is, a collective, universal (common), and powerful Will —is the kind of Will that can provide the guarantee required. The condition of being subject to general external (that is, public) legislation that is backed by power is the civil society. Accordingly, a thing can be externally yours or mine only in a civil society.

Conclusion: If it must be *de jure* possible to have an external object as one's own, then the subject must also be allowed to compel everyone else with whom he comes into conflict over the question of whether such an object is his to enter, together with him, a society under a civil constitution.

§ 9. IN THE STATE OF NATURE, THERE CAN BE ACTUAL EXTERNAL PROPERTY, BUT IT IS ONLY PROVISIONAL

In a society under a civil constitution, natural Law (that is, that kind of Law that can be derived for such a society from a priori principles) cannot be abrogated by the statutory laws of that society. Consequently, the juridical principle remains in force: "He who acts from a maxim according to which it becomes impossible for me to have an object of my will as mine thereby injures me." A civil constitution only provides the juridical condition under which each person's property is secured and guaranteed to him, but it does not actually stipulate and determine what that property shall be.

Thus, the guarantee itself already presupposes the property of someone (to whom it is guaranteed). Therefore, external property—what is yours and mine—must be assumed to be possible prior to the civil constitution (or without taking it into account). Along with it goes a right to compel everyone with whom we might have any kind of intercourse to enter, together with us, a society under a constitution where the security of external property can be guaranteed.

257   Possession in expectation and preparation for a civil society, which can only be founded on a law of the common Will—if such possession is consistent with the possibility of such a law —is *provisional de jure* possession. In contrast to this, possession found in an actual civil society is *peremptory* possession.

Before entering a civil society, if the subject is ready and willing to enter it, then he rightfully [*mit Recht*] resists those who do not put up with it and want to disturb him in his temporary possession. [He can do this rightfully] because, if the Will of all others beside him proposes to impose an obligation on him to abandon a particular possession, it is still a merely unilateral Will, and as such it has exactly as little lawful force to deny his possession as he, for his part, has to assert it (for lawful force is to be found only in the general Will). In the meantime, the person in question has the advantage over the rest in that he agrees to the introduction and establishment of a civil society.

In one word, the mode of having something external as one's own property in a state of nature is physical possession, which carries with it the juridical presumption that, through the union of the Will of everyone in public legislation, this possession will be made into *de jure* possession. In the preparatory period preceding the civil society, such possession is taken as comparatively *de jure*.

This prerogative of a right based on empirical possession, in accordance with the formula, "Happy is he who is in possession" *(beati possidentes)*, is not based on the presumption that the person in question is an honest man, so that it is unnecessary for him to prove that he possesses something legitimately (for that kind of argument is acceptable only in litigation [*im streitigen Rechte*]). Instead, [this principle] follows from the postulate of practical reason according to which everyone has the capacity to have an external object of his will as his own property. Hence, detention is always a state of affairs whose legitimacy is founded on that postulate through an act of Will preceding it [that is, detention], and, as long as this detention does not conflict with someone else's more ancient possession of the same object, it is a state of affairs that, in accordance with the law of external freedom, provisionally justifies preventing anyone who refuses to enter with me the condition of public lawful freedom [that is, the civil society] from usurping use of the object. Thus, in conformity with the postulate of reason, he subjects to his own use something that would otherwise be reduced to nought from the practical point of view.[12]

---

[12] [The sections that follow, §§ 10–35, are omitted, as being mainly concerned with technical concepts belonging to eighteenth-century German law. These concepts are derived from Roman law and do not have any exact counterparts in Anglo-American law. Hence they are of little interest except to the specialist. The philosophical remarks contained in these sections merely repeat what is said elsewhere in the text. The headings are as follows:

Second Chapter:
Of the Mode of Acquiring Something External

§ 10—The General Principle of External Acquisition. Division of [Types of] Acquisition of External Property.

First Section: Rights *in rem*. § 11—What Is a Real Right (*jus reale*)? § 12—First Acquisition of a Thing Can Be Nothing Else Than the Acquisition of Land. § 13—Every Piece of Land Can Be Acquired Originally, and the Ground of the Possibility of This Kind of Acquisition Is the Original Community of Land in General. § 14—The Juridical Act of This Acquisition Is Occupation (*occupatio*). § 15—A Thing Can Be Acquired Peremptorily Only Under a Civil Constitution; It Can Also Be Acquired in the State of Nature, but Only Provisionally. § 16—Exposition of the Concept of Original Acquisition of Land. § 17—Deduction of the Concept of Original Acquisition.

Second Section: Rights *in personam*. §18–21—[Contracts].

Third Section: Rights *in rem* over Persons. § 22–23—[General].

The law of domestic society. § 24–27—First Title: Marital Rights. § 28–29—Second Title: Parental Rights. § 30—Third Title: Rights of a Master

✒ third chapter ✒
OF ACQUISITION THAT IS SUBJECTIVELY
STIPULATED THROUGH A DECISION
OF A PUBLIC JUDICIARY [*Gerichtsbarkeit*]

§ 36

297   If natural justice is only conceived as nonstatutory Law,
that is, simply the Law that can be known a priori by every
human being, then not only will the legal justice that per-
tains to mutual dealings of persons with one another (*justitia
commutativa*) belong to it, but also distributive legal justice
(*justitia distributiva*), so far as its law can be known a priori—
the law according to which a judicial decision has to be rendered.

A moral person[1] who administers legal justice is a court
of law [*Gerichtshof*] (*forum*), and the process of administering
the office is a trial [*Gericht*] (*judicium*). These are a priori conceptions following from the conditions of justice itself, without regard to how a particular constitution is to be set up and
organized (for the latter involves statutes, that is, empirical
principles).

Therefore, the question that arises here is not simply: What
is just in itself, that is, how does every human being have to
judge concerning it? Rather it is; What is just before a court
of law, that is, what is Lawful [that is, required by the laws of
the country]? Now, there are four cases in which these two
kinds of judgment differ and are opposed to one another, yet
can coexist, for they are made from two different but equally

---

over His Servant. § 31—Dogmatic Division of All Rights Acquirable
Through Contract. I—What Is Money? II—What Is a Book?

§ 32—Episodic Section: Concerning Ideal Acquisition of an External Object of the Will. § 33—I—Acquisition Through Occupancy. § 34—II—Inheritance. § 35—III—The Legacy of a Good Name.

[1] [By "moral person," Kant means an artificial—for example, legal—
person. Thus, a court that consists of several judges may be considered
one "moral person." See note 4, § 48, below.]

true points of view—one from the point of view of private Law; the other, from the point of view of the Idea of public Law. These four cases are: (1) a gift contract *(pactum donationis)*; (2) a loan contract *(commodatum)*; (3) recovery *(vindicatio)*; and (4) the administration of oaths *(juramentum)*.

Teachers of law commonly misrepresent the juridical principle that a court of law, for its own special purposes (hence from a subjective point of view), is authorized, nay, bound to adopt in order to deliberate and judge concerning the right due someone by holding this principle to be something that is also objectively just in itself. This is a fallacy *(vitium subreptionis)*,[2] inasmuch as the former differs greatly from the latter. It is therefore of no slight importance to make known and to call attention to the specific difference between them.[3]

TRANSITION FROM PROPERTY IN A STATE OF NATURE TO PROPERTY IN A JURIDICAL STATE IN GENERAL

§ 41

A juridical state of affairs is a relationship among human beings that involves the conditions under which alone every man is able to enjoy his right. The formal principle of the possibility of this state of affairs, regarded as the Idea of a general legislative Will, is called public legal justice. Public legal justice can be divided into three parts as it relates to the possibility, actuality, and necessity of the possession of objects in accordance with laws.[4] (These objects are the content [matter]

306

---

2 ["Fallacy of deception."]

3 [The following sections are omitted. A. § 37—Of Gift Contracts. B. § 38—Of Loan Contracts. C. § 39—Of the Recovery of What Has Been Lost *(vindicatio)*. D. § 40—Of the Securing of a Guarantee by Means of Oaths *(cautio juratoria)*.]

4 [*Nach Gesetzen*. The structure of the German sentence is ambiguous, so that other translations might be "divided according to laws," or "these parts separated according to laws."]

of the will.) These three parts are protective, reciprocally acquisitive, and distributive legal justice, respectively (*justitia tutatrix, justitia commutativa, justitia distributiva*).

Thus law [*das Gesetz*] sets forth: first, simply what [kind of] conduct is inwardly just as regards its form (*lex justi*); second, in regard to its matter, what [things] are capable of [being objects] of external legislation [*gesetzfähig*], that is, the possession of which is juridically right (*lex juridica*); third, what, before a court of law, is the decision that accords with a given law with regard to a particular case coming under law, that is, what the actual Law of the land (*lex justitiae*) is.[5] Whence a court of law itself is called the "justice" of a country, and, as it is the most important of all juridical concerns, one can ask whether this kind of justice exists or not.

A nonjuridical state of affairs, that is, one in which there is no distributive legal justice, is called the state of nature (*status naturalis*). The state of nature is not (as Achenwall [6] thought) to be contrasted to living in society, which might be called an artificial state of affairs (*status artificialis*); rather, it is to be contrasted to civil society, where society stands under distributive justice. Even in a state of nature, there can be legitimate societies (for example, conjugal, paternal, domestic groups in general, and many others) concerning which there is no a priori law declaring: "Thou shalt enter into this condition." On the other hand, it can indeed be said of the juridical state of affairs that all men ought to enter it if they ever could (even involuntarily) come into a relationship with one another that involves mutual rights [or justice] [*Rechtsverhältnisse*].

The first and second of these states of affairs can be called

[5] [The German terms corresponding to these three kinds of law are *recht, rechtlich,* and *Rechtens.*]

[6] [Gottfried Achenwall (1719–1772), a German political scientist. For many years, Kant used Achenwall's book *Jus naturae in usum auditorum* (1767) as a textbook in his lectures on natural law. Part II of this work is reproduced in its entirety in Volume XIX of Kant's *Gesammelte Schriften* (Akademie Ausgabe).]

the state of private Law, whereas the third and last can be called the state of public Law. Public Law does not involve any additional or different duties among men than can be thought of under private Law; the matter [that is, the substance] of private Law is exactly the same in both. The laws of public Law are concerned only with the juridical form of men living together (the constitution), in respect to which these laws must necessarily be thought of as public laws.

A civil union itself cannot even be called a society, for between a commander (*imperans*) and his subject (*subditus*) there is no coequal partnership. They are not associates, for one is subordinate rather than coordinate to the other. For the same reason, those who are coordinate to one another must regard themselves as equal among themselves insofar as they are subject to common laws. The civil union does not, therefore, constitute a society, but rather produces one.

307

§ 42

The postulate of public Law comes out of private Law in the state of nature. It says: If you are so situated as to be unavoidably side by side with others, you ought to abandon the state of nature and enter, with all others, a juridical state of affairs, that is, a state of distributive legal justice. The ground of this postulate can be developed analytically from the concept of justice in external relations, as contrasted to violence (*violentia*).

No one is bound to refrain from encroaching on the possession of another man if the latter does not in equal measure guarantee that the same kind of restraint will be exercised with regard to him. Therefore, he need not wait until he finds out through bitter experience about the hostile attitude of the other man. There is nothing binding him to wait to become prudent until after he has suffered a loss. Because he can quite adequately observe within himself the inclination of mankind in general to play the master over others (that is, man's inclination not to respect the rights of others when he feels superior to them in might or cleverness), it is unnecessary to wait for actual hostilities. A man is authorized to use coercion against anyone who by his very nature threatens him. (*Quilibet praesumitur malus, donec securitatem dederit oppositi.*[7])

If men deliberately and intentionally resolve to be in and to remain in this state of external lawless freedom, then they cannot wrong each other by fighting among themselves; for whatever goes for one of them goes reciprocally for the other as though they had made an agreement to that effect (*uti partes de jure suo disponunt, ita jus est*[8]). Nevertheless, in general they act in the highest degree wrongly by wanting to be in and to remain in a state that is not juridical, that is, a state of affairs in which no one is secure in what belongs to him against deeds of violence.[9]

308

---

[7] ["Everyone is presumed bad until he has provided assurance of the opposite."]

[8] ["As the parties decide their own right, so the right is."]

[9] The distinction between what is wrong [or unjust] merely formally and what is wrong [or unjust] also materially has many applications in jurisprudence. If, instead of honorably carrying out his surrender agreement with the garrison of a besieged fortress, an enemy abuses the men as they march out or in some other way violates the agreement, then he cannot complain of any wrong [or injustice] when his adversary seizes the opportunity to play the same trick on him. Nevertheless, in general they do what is in the highest degree wrong, for they rob the concept of justice itself of all its validity and deliver everything over to wild violence as though this were itself legal, thus subverting the right of mankind in general.

308

II
PUBLIC LAW

✒ *second part* ✒
PUBLIC LAW

✒ *first section* ✒
MUNICIPAL LAW [1]

§ 43 [DEFINITION OF PUBLIC LAW]

The body of those laws that require public promulgation in order to produce a juridical condition is called *public Law.* Public Law is therefore a system of laws for a nation—that is, a multitude of men—or for a multitude of nations. In order to be able to participate in the actual Law of the land, these men and nations require, because they mutually influence one another, a juridical condition of society. That is, they require a condition of society under a Will that unites them—a constitution.

When the individuals within a nation are related to one another in this way, they constitute a *civil society (status civilis)*; and, viewed as a whole in relation to its own members, this civil society is called *the state (civitas).* Because the state is by its very form a union proceeding from the common interest of all in having a juridical condition of society, it is called a *commonwealth (res publica latius sic dicta).* In relation to other nations, however, a state is called simply a power *(potentia)*—hence the word "potentate." When there is a pretense of common heredity, it is also called a nationality or race [*Stammvolk*] *(gens).* Hence, not only municipal Law, but also a Law of nations [*Völkerrecht*] *(jus gentium)* may be thought of as belonging to the general concept of public Law. Because the surface of the earth is not unlimited in extent, both kinds of Law inevitably lead to the Idea of international Law [*Völkerstaatsrecht*] *(jus gentium)* or of world Law [*Weltbürgerrecht*] *(jus cosmopoliticum).*

1 [*Staatsrecht.* In contrast to international law, municipal law is that of an individual state or nation.]

Consequently, if just one of these possible forms of juridical condition lacks a principle circumscribing external freedom through laws, then the structure of all the others will unavoidably be undermined and must finally collapse.

312   § 44 [RIGHTS IN A STATE OF NATURE]

Although experience teaches us that men live in violence and are prone to fight one another before the advent of external compulsive legislation, it is not experience that makes public lawful coercion necessary. The necessity of public lawful coercion does not rest on a fact, but on an a priori Idea of reason, for, even if we imagine men to be ever so good natured and righteous before a public lawful state of society is established, individual men, nations, and states can never be certain that they are secure against violence from one another, because each will have his own right to do what *seems just and good to him,* entirely independently of the opinion of others. Consequently, the first decision that he must make, if he does not wish to renounce all concepts of justice, is to accept the principle that one must quit the state of nature, in which everyone follows his own judgment, and must unite with everyone else (with whom he comes in contact and whom he cannot avoid), subjecting himself to a public lawful external coercion; in other words, he must enter a condition of society in which what is to be recognized as belonging to him must be established lawfully and secured to him by an effective power that is not his own, but an outside power. That is, before anything else, he ought to enter a civil society.

Certainly, a state of nature need not be a condition of injustice [*Ungerechtigkeit*] *(injustus)* in which men treat one another solely according to the amount of power they possess; it is, however, still a state of society in which justice is absent [*Rechtlosigkeit*] *(status justitiae vacuus)* and one in which, when there is a controversy concerning rights *(jus controversum)*, no competent judge can be found to render a decision having the force of law. For this reason, everyone may use violent means to compel another to enter into a juridical state of society. Although according to everyone's concept of justice and right an external thing can be acquired by occupation or by contract, such acquisition is still only provisional as long as there is no sanction of a public law for it, for the acquisition is not determined by any public legal (distributive) justice and is not guaranteed by any authority executing the Law.

If it were held that no acquisition, not even provisional acquisition, is juridically valid before the establishment of a civil society, then the civil society itself would be impossible. This follows from the fact that, as regards their form, the laws concerning property in a state of nature contain the same things that are prescribed by the laws in civil society insofar as they are considered merely as pure concepts of reason; the only difference is that, in the civil society, the conditions are given under which the [right of] acquisition can be exercised (in conformity with distributive legal justice). Accordingly, if there were not even provisional property in a state of nature, there would be no duties of justice with respect to them, and, consequently, there would be no command to quit the state of nature.

313

§ 45 [THE CIVIL STATE]

A state (*civitas*) is a union of a multitude of men under laws of justice. Insofar as these laws are necessary a priori and follow from the concepts of external justice in general (that is, are not established by statute), the form of the state is that of a state in general, that is, the Idea of the state as it ought to be according to pure principles of justice. This Idea provides an internal guide and standard (*norma*) [2] for every actual union of men in a commonwealth.

[2] [The German reads: ". . . (also im Inneren) zur Richtschnur." I believe that Kant's point is that the principles of justice can function as motives in themselves only when regarded as inner ethical precepts. See Translator's Introduction, pp. xiii–xiv.]

Every state contains within itself three authorities, that is, the general united Will is composed of three persons (*trias politica*). The sovereign authority resides in the person of the legislator; the executive authority resides in the person of the ruler (in conformity to law), and the judicial authority (which assigns to everyone what is his own by law) resides in the person of the judge (*potestas legislatoria, rectoria, et judiciaria*). These three parts are like the three propositions in a practical syllogism: the law of the sovereign Will is like the major premise; the command to act according to the law is like the minor premise that is the principle of subsumption under the Will; and the adjudication (the sentence) that establishes what the actual Law of the land in the case under consideration is, is like the conclusion.

§ 46 [THE LEGISLATIVE AUTHORITY AND THE CITIZEN]

The legislative authority can be attributed only to the united Will of the people. Because all right and justice is supposed to proceed from this authority, it can do absolutely no injustice to anyone. Now, when someone prescribes for another, it is always possible that he thereby does the other an injustice, but this is never possible with respect to what he decides for himself (for *volenti non fit injuria*).[3] Hence, only the united and consenting Will of all—that is, a general united Will of the people by which each decides the same for all and all decide the same for each—can legislate.

314

The members of such a society (*societas civilis*), that is, of a state, who are united for the purpose of making laws are called *citizens* (*cives*). There are three juridical attributes inseparably bound up with the nature of a citizen as such: first, the lawful freedom to obey no law other than one to which he has given his consent, second, the civil equality of having among the people no superior over him except another person whom he has just as much of a moral capacity to bind jurid-

---

3 ["He who consents cannot receive an injury."]

ically as the other has to bind him; third, the attribute of
civil independence that requires that he owe his existence and
support, not to the arbitrary will of another person in the
society, but rather to his own rights and powers as a member
of the commonwealth (hence his own civil personality may
not be represented by another person in matters involving justice and rights).

Fitness for voting is a prerequisite of being a citizen.
To be fit to vote, a person must be independent and not
just a part of the commonwealth, but also a member of it,
that is, he must will of his own accord, together with
others, to be an active part of the commonwealth. This
qualification leads to the distinction between an active
and a passive citizen, although the concept of the latter
appears to contradict the definition of the concept of a
citizen in general. The following examples [of passive
citizens] may serve to clear up this difficulty: an appren-
tice of a merchant or artisan; a servant (not in the service
of the state); a minor (*naturaliter vel civiliter*); all women;
and generally anyone who must depend for his support
(subsistence and protection), not on his own industry,
but on arrangements by others (with the exception of the
state)—all such people lack civil personality, and their
existence is only in the mode of inherence. The woodcut-
ter whom I employ on my estate; the smith in India who
goes with his hammer, anvil, and bellows into houses to
work on iron, in contrast to the European carpenter or
smith, who can offer the products of his labor for public   315
sale; the private tutor, in contrast to the schoolteacher;
the sharecropper, in contrast to the farmer; and the like—
all are mere underlings of the commonwealth, because
they must be under the orders or protection of other individuals. Consequently, they do not possess any civil independence.

This kind of dependence on the Will of others and
the inequality that it involves are by no means incompatible with the freedom and equality that men possess as

human beings, who together make up a people. Rather, only by conforming to these conditions can the people become a state and enter into a civil constitution. Under this constitution, however, not everyone is equally qualified to have the right to vote, that is, to be a citizen as well as a fellow subject [Staatsgenosse]. From the fact that, as passive parts of the state, they can still demand that they be treated by others in accordance with the laws of natural freedom and equality it does not follow that they have the right as active members to guide the state, to organize, and to work for the introduction of particular laws; it follows only that, whatever might be the kind of laws to which the citizens agree, these laws must not be incompatible with the natural laws of freedom and with the equality that accords with this freedom, namely, that everyone be able to work up from this passive status to an active status.

§ 47 [THE ORIGINAL CONTRACT]

All the three authorities in the state are dignities, and, inasmuch as it follows from the Idea of the state in general that they are necessary to the formation of a state (constitution), they are public or civil dignities [Staatswürden]. They embody the relationship of a universal suzerain (who, if regarded under the laws of freedom, can be none other than the united people) to the aggregate of individuals regarded as subjects, that is, the relationship of commander (imperans) to one who obeys (subditus). The act by means of which the people constitute themselves a state is the original contract. More properly, it is the Idea of that act that alone enables us to conceive of the legitimacy of the state. According to the original contract, all (omnes et singuli) the people give up their external freedom in order to take it back again immediately as members of a commonwealth, that is, the people regarded as the 316 state (universi). Accordingly, we cannot say that a man has sacrificed in the state a part of his inborn external freedom for some particular purpose; rather, we must say that he has completely abandoned his wild, lawless freedom in order to find his whole freedom again undiminished in a lawful dependency, that is, in a juridical state of society, since this dependency comes from his own legislative Will.

§ 48 [MUTUAL RELATIONSHIPS OF THE THREE AUTHORITIES]

The three authorities in the state are related to one another in the following ways: First, considered as three moral persons,[4] they are coordinate (*potestates coordinatae*); that is, one serves as a complement to the others for the completeness of the state's constitution (*complementum ad sufficientiam*). Second, they are subordinate to one another so that one cannot at the same time usurp the function of the others which are there to aid it. Instead, each has its own proper principle; that is, although it commands when considered in its quality as a particular person, it does so only under the condition of the Will of a superior person. Third, the combination of both relationships secures to every subject what is just and right.[5]

Of these authorities considered in their dignity, we can say: the Will of the legislator (*legislatoris*) with respect to external property is irreproachable (*irreprehensibel*); the executive capacity of the chief magistrate is irresistible (*irresistibel*); and the adjudication of the supreme judge (*supremi judicis*) is unalterable (*inappellabel*).

§ 49 [THE EXECUTIVE AUTHORITY AND THE DISTINCT FUNCTIONS OF THE THREE AUTHORITIES]

The *ruler* of the state (*rex, princeps*) is that (moral or physical) person who has the executive authority (*potestas executoria*). He is the agent of the state who appoints the magis-

[4] [By "moral person," Kant means what we would call an artificial person (for example, a corporation), and by "physical person" he means a natural person. See note 1, § 36, above.]

[5] [Natorp and Cassirer agree that part of the text is missing here.]

trates and prescribes those rules for the people by means of which each of them can, in conformity with the law, acquire things or preserve his property (by subsumption of one case under the law). If the ruler is regarded as a moral person, he is called the directory or the government. The commands that he gives to the people, the magistrates, and the ministers who are in charge of the administration (*gubernatio*) are not laws, but ordinances and decrees, because they involve decisions about particular cases and are considered subject to change. A government that at the same time makes laws would be called

317   *despotic,* in contrast to a *patriotic* government. A patriotic government should not be confused with a paternal government (*regimen paternale*), which is the most despotic of all, for it treats its citizens as children. In a patriotic government (*regimen civitatis et patriae*), the state itself does indeed treat its subjects as members of a family, but at the same time it also treats them as citizens of the state, that is, in accordance with laws of their own proper independence; and everyone possesses himself and does not depend on the absolute Will of another next to or over him.

Therefore, the sovereign [*Beherrscher*] of the people (the legislator) cannot at the same time be the ruler, for the ruler is himself subject to the law and through it is obligated to another, the sovereign. The sovereign can take his authority from the ruler, depose him, or reform his administration, but cannot punish him. (That is the only meaning that can be given to the common saying in England: "The King, that is, the supreme executive authority, can do no wrong.") The ruler cannot be punished because to punish him would itself in turn be an act of the executive authority, to which alone belongs the supreme capacity to use coercion in accordance with the law. To punish the ruler would mean that the highest executive authority itself would be subject to coercion, which is a self-contradiction.

Finally, neither the sovereign nor the ruler can judge; they can only appoint judges as magistrates. The people judge themselves through those of their fellow citizens whom they have named by free elections as their representatives and whom they have named, indeed, specially for each act. An adjudication (a sentence) is an individual act of public legal justice (*justitiae distributivae*) performed by an official of the state (judge or court of justice) on a subject, that is, on someone belonging to the people. Consequently, as such, the act is not invested with any authority to allot or assign property to the subject. Because each person among the people is purely passive in relation to the supreme power, if either the legislative or the executive authority were to decide in a controversial case concerning his property, it might do him an injustice, for it would not be the people themselves acting or saying that their fellow citizen is guilty or not guilty. But, once the facts in a legal suit have been established, then a court of justice has the judicial authority to apply the law and to render, through the mediation of the executive authority, to each person what is his due, his property. Therefore, only the people can judge one of themselves, although they do this indirectly by means of their delegated representatives (the jury). It would also be beneath the dignity of the chief of state to perform the function of judge, because this would 318 put him in a position in which it would be possible to do an injustice and thus to subject himself to the demand for an appeal to a higher authority (*a rege male informato ad regem melius informandum*).[6]

Thus there are three distinct authorities (*potestas legislatoria, executoria, judiciaria*) by means of which the state (*civitas*) acquires its autonomy, that is, by means of which it forms and maintains itself in accordance with the laws of freedom. The state's well-being consists in their being united (*salus reipublicae suprema lex est*).[7] But the well-being of the state must not be confused with the welfare or happiness of the citizens of the state, for these can be attained more easily and satisfactorily in a state of nature (as Rousseau main-

---

[6] ["From a king poorly informed to a king who ought to be better informed."]

[7] ["The welfare of the commonwealth is the supreme law."]

tained) or even under a despotic government. By "the well-being of the state" is meant that condition in which the constitution conforms most closely to the principles of justice, that is, the condition that reason through a categorical imperative obligates us to strive after.

GENERAL REMARKS ON THE JURIDICAL CONSEQUENCES ARISING FROM THE NATURE OF THE CIVIL UNION

A [Revolution, Resistance, and Reform]

The origin of the supreme authority is, from the practical point of view, not open to scrutiny by the people who are subject to it; that is, the subject should not be overly curious about its origin as though the right of obedience due it were open to doubt (jus controversum). For in order for the people to be able to judge the supreme political authority (summum imperium) with the force of law, they must already be viewed as united under a general legislative Will; hence they can and may not judge otherwise than the present chief of state wills (summus imperans). Whether as a historical fact an actual contract between them originally preceded the submission to authority (pactum subjectionis civilis) or whether, instead, the authority preceded it and the law only came later or even is supposed to have followed in this order—these are pointless questions that threaten the state with danger if they are asked with too much sophistication by a people who are already subject to civil law; for, if the subject decides to resist the present ruling authority as the result of ruminating on its origin, he would be rightfully punished, destroyed, or exiled (as an outlaw, exlex) in accordance with the laws of that authority itself.

A law that is so holy and inviolable that it is a crime even to doubt it or to suspend it for an instant is represented as coming, not from mankind, but from some highest perfect legislator. That is the meaning of the statement, "All ruling power comes from God," which is not a historical explanation of the civil constitution, but an Idea that expresses the practi-

cal principle of reason that one ought to obey the legislative
authority that now exists, regardless of its origin.

From this follows the statement: the sovereign in the state
has many rights with respect to the subject, but no (coercive)
duties. Furthermore, if the organ of the sovereign, the ruler,
proceeds contrary to the laws—for example, in imposing taxes,
recruiting soldiers, and so on, so as to violate the law of equality in the distribution of political burdens—the subject may
lodge a complaint (*gravamina*) about this injustice, but he
may not actively resist.

Indeed, even the constitution itself cannot contain any
article that would allow for some authority in the state that
could resist or restrain the chief magistrate in cases in which
he violates the constitutional laws. For he who is supposed to
restrain the authority of the state must have more power
than, or at least as much power as, the person whom he is
supposed to restrain, and, as a legitimate commander, if he
orders his subjects to resist, he must also be able to protect
them and to render a judgment having the force of law in any
particular case that arises; in other words, he must be able to
command the resistance publicly. But then the latter would be
the chief magistrate, not the former; and this supposition contradicts itself. In this case, the sovereign is, through his minister, at the same time acting as a ruler, and is therefore acting
despotically; the hocus-pocus of letting the people (who properly have only legislative authority) imagine that they are
limiting the authority through their deputies cannot succeed
in covering up the despotism so that it will not be obvious in
the methods that the minister employs. The deputies who
represent the people (in parliament) and who act as guarantors
of their freedom and rights have a lively personal interest in
positions for themselves and their families; and, inasmuch as
these depend on the minister—as in the army, navy, or civil
bureaucracy—these deputies are always much more ready to   320
play into the hands of the administration (instead of resisting
the encroachment of the government). (Besides, the public
promulgation of such resistance requires an already existent

unanimity among the people concerning it, but such unanimity cannot be permitted in time of peace.)

It follows that a so-called moderate political constitution [*gemässigte Staatsverfassung*], representing itself as the constitution of the internal justice and Law of the state, is nonsense and that, instead of being a part of justice and Law, it is a clever principle devised to make the arbitrary influence on the government of a powerful transgressor of the people's rights as little onerous as possible by cloaking it in the appearance of conceding to the people [the right of] opposition.

There can therefore be no legitimate resistance of the people to the legislative chief of the state; for juridical status, legitimacy, is possible only through subjection to the general legislative Will of the people. Accordingly, there is no right of sedition (*seditio*), much less a right of revolution (*rebellio*), and least of all a right to lay hands on or take the life of the chief of state when he is an individual person on the excuse that he has misused his authority (*tyrannis, monarchomachismus sub specie tyrannicidii*). The slightest attempt to do this is high treason (*proditio eminens*), and a traitor of this kind, as someone attempting to destroy his fatherland (*parricida*), can receive no lesser punishment than death.

It is the people's duty to endure even the most intolerable abuse of supreme authority. The reason for this is that resistance to the supreme legislation can itself only be unlawful; indeed it must be conceived as destroying the entire lawful constitution, because, in order for it to be authorized, there would have to be a public law that would permit the resistance. That is, the supreme legislation would have to contain a stipulation that it is not supreme and that in one and the same judgment the people as subjects should be made sovereign over him to whom they are subject; this is self-contradictory. The self-contradiction involved here is immediately evident if we ask who would act as judge in this controversy between the people and the sovereign (because, regarded juridically, they are still two distinct moral persons). [In such a controversy] it is plain that the people want to act as judge of their own cause [and that is absurd].[8]

8 It is conceivable that the dethronement of a monarch may be effected either through a voluntary abdication of the crown and a renunciation of his authority by returning it to the people or through a relinquishment of authority carried out without laying hands on the highest person, who thereafter returns to the status of a private citizen. Consequently, the people might have at least some excuse for forcibly bringing this about by appealing to the right of necessity (*casus necessitatis*), but they never have the least right to punish the suzerain for his previous administration, inasmuch as everything that he previously did in his role of suzerain must be regarded as having been externally legitimate; and, because he is regarded as the source of the laws, he cannot himself do an injustice. Of all the abominations involved in the overthrow of a state through revolution, the murder of the monarch is still not the worst, because it is possible to imagine that the people are motivated by the fear that, were he to remain alive, he might regain his power and give them the punishment they deserve; in that case, this deed would not be an act of penal justice, but only one of self-preservation. It is the formal execution of a monarch that fills the soul, conscious of the Ideas of human justice, with horror, and this horror returns whenever one thinks of scenes like those in which the fate of Charles I or Louis XVI was sealed. How can this feeling be explained? It is not an aesthetic feeling (of the kind of compassion that results from imagining oneself in the place of the sufferer), but a moral feeling arising from the complete subversion of every concept of justice. It is regarded as a crime that remains eternally and cannot be expiated (*crimen immortale, inexpiabile*), and it appears to resemble the kind of sin that, according to theologians, can never be forgiven in this world or the next. The explanation of this phenomenon of the human spirit seems to emerge from the following reflections on oneself, and these reflections also throw some light on the principles of political justice [*staatsrechtlichen Prinzipien*].

Every transgression of the law can and must be explained only as arising from the maxim of the criminal (the maxim of making such a misdeed into a rule), for, were it to be derived from a sensible impulse, it would not be committed by the agent himself as a free being and could not be imputed to him. It is absolutely impossible to explain how a subject can form a maxim in opposition to the clear prohibition of legislative reason, for only events in the mechanism of nature are susceptible of explanation. Now, the criminal can commit the misdeed either by following a maxim of a presumed objective rule (supposed to be universally valid) or as an exception to the rule (by dispensing with it for the occasion). In the latter case, he only strays from the law (even though intentionally); he

321   An alteration in a (defective) constitution of a state, which
        may sometimes be required, can be undertaken only by the
322   sovereign himself through reform, and not by the people
        through a revolution. Moreover, such an alteration should af-
        fect only the executive authority, not the legislative authority.
            Even in what is called a limited constitution [*eingeschränkte
        Verfassung*], that is, in a constitution of a state in which the
        people through their representatives (in parliament) can law-
        fully oppose the executive or his representative (his minister),
        no active resistance is permitted—no resistance, that is, in
        which an arbitrary association of the people coerces the gov-
        ernment into acting in a certain way, for this would be arro-

        can at the same time detest his own transgression, and he can still want
        to circumvent the law without formally renouncing his obedience to it.
        In the former case, however, he repudiates the authority of the law it-
        self, even though he cannot deny its validity before his own reason; his
322   maxim is not merely deficient (*negative*) with respect to the law, but is
        even contrary (*contrarie*) to it, or, we might say, it is diametrically op-
        posed to it as a contradiction (hostile, as it were). Thus, it is clear to
        us that to commit a crime of such formal (completely useless) malevolence
        is impossible for any man and cannot be introduced into a system of
        morality (except as the pure Idea of extreme perversity).
            The reason why the thought of a formal execution of a monarch by
        his people is so horrible is that, whereas a murder must be conceived of
        only as an exception to the rule, a formal execution must be conceived
        of as a complete subversion of the principles governing the relationship
        between a sovereign and his people (that is, it makes the people the
        master over the former, to whose legislation alone they owe their ex-
        istence). Accordingly, the employment of violence is brazenly and de-
        liberately [*nach Grundsätzen*] placed above the holiest right and justice;
        as such, it is like being swallowed up in an abyss from which there is
        no return, like the state's committing suicide, and so it appears to be
        a crime that is incapable of being expiated. There is good reason to be-
        lieve, therefore, that assent to such executions is not really based on a
        supposed juridical principle, but rather on the fear of revenge by the
        state, which might perhaps revive again, and that these formalities are
        adopted merely in order to give the deed the semblance of an act of pun-
        ishment, a juridical process (which could not be murder). But such a dis-
        guise will do no good, inasmuch as this kind of arrogant usurpation on
        the part of the people is much more heinous than murder itself, for it
        contains within itself a principle that must make impossible the restora-
        tion of a state that has been overthrown.

gating to itself an act of the executive authority. A limited constitution permits only a negative resistance, that is, a refusal by the people (in parliament) to accede always to the demands of the executive authority with regard to what the latter alleges to be required for the administration of the state. Indeed, if these demands were always acceded to, we would have a sure sign that the people are corrupt, their representatives venal, the chief of the government through his minister despotic, and the minister himself a betrayer of the people.

Moreover, if a revolution has succeeded and a new constitution has been established, the illegitimacy of its beginning and of its success cannot free the subjects from being bound to accept the new order of things as good citizens, and they cannot refuse to honor and obey the suzerain [*Obrigkeit*] who now possesses the authority. The dethroned monarch (who survives such a revolution) cannot be held accountable for, much less be punished for, his past administration, provided that he has retired to the private life of a citizen of the state and prefers peace and quiet for himself and the state to the foolhardy act of running away in order, as a pretender, to attempt the adventure of recovering his kingdom, whether it be through a secretly instigated counterrevolution or through the help of outside powers. If, however, he prefers the latter course of action, his right to do so remains unchallengeable, because the insurrection that deprived him of his possession was unjust [*ungerecht*]. But whether other powers have the right to join in an alliance in favor of this dethroned monarch merely so that this crime of his people shall not go unpunished and so remain a scandal to all other states and whether they are therefore justified and called upon to use their authority and power to restore the old constitution in every state where a new constitution has been set up as the result of a revolution—these are questions that come under the Law of nations.[9]

323

9 [See Appendix, Conclusion, pp. 138–141 below, for additional remarks on the subject of revolution.]

B [*The Sovereign as Supreme Proprietor of the Land—*
Taxation—Police—Inspection]

Can the sovereign be regarded as the supreme proprietor (of the land), or must he be regarded only as the person who exercises supreme command over the people by virtue of the laws? Because [the existence of] land provides the chief necessary condition of the possibility of having external things as one's property and establishes the first acquirable right of possible possession and use, all such rights must be derived from the sovereign as the lord of the land or, better put, the supreme proprietor (*dominus territorii*). The people, as the aggregate of his subjects, also belong to him; they are his people. But he is not their owner (by a right *in rem*); rather, he is their supreme commander (by a right *in personam*).

This supreme proprietorship is, however, only an Idea of the civil union that serves the purpose of representing the necessary unification of the private property of all the people under a public general possessor, so that the determination of particular owners is in accordance with the necessary formal principle of division (division of the land) in terms of concepts of justice, rather than by principles of aggregation (which proceed empirically from part to whole). Accordingly, the supreme proprietor cannot privately own any land (for otherwise he would become a private person), and all land belongs to the people (not collectively, but distributively). (An exception to this is to be found in nomadic tribes, where there is no private ownership of land.) Therefore, the supreme commander can have no private estates, that is, lands for his private use (for the maintenance of his court), for, if he did, since the limits and extent of his lands would depend on his own pleasure and discretion, the state would be in danger of having all ownership of the land pass into the hands of the government, and all the subjects would be considered bondsmen of the soil (*glebae adscripti*) and possessors of what is owned only by someone else. They would consequently be regarded as having lost all their freedom (*servi*). Accordingly, one can say of the lord of a country [*Landesherr*] that *he possesses nothing* (as his own) except himself, since, if he were to own anything adjacent to someone else in the state, a dispute might arise between them, and there would be no judge to settle it. But one can also say: *he possesses everything* because he has the right of command over the people, to whom all external things belong (*divisum*) (and by this right he assigns to each person what is his own).

From this it follows that there can be no corporation, class, or order in the state that as owners can under certain statutes transmit lands to succeeding generations for their sole and exclusive use (for all time). The state can at all times rescind such statutes, but only on condition that it compensates the survivors. The knightly order (considered as a corporation or even just as the rank of specially honored individual persons) and the order of the clergy, which is called the church, can never acquire ownership in land that is transmissible to their successors by virtue of the privileges with which they are favored; they can acquire only its temporary use. The military orders, on the one hand, can be deprived of their estates without hesitation (except for the condition mentioned above) if public opinion no longer wants to use them as a means of defending the state by conferring military honors in order to overcome indifference to its defense. The churches, on the other hand, can similarly be deprived of their estates if public opinion does not want to use them to save the people of the state from eternal fire by means of masses for departed souls, prayer, and a multitude of clergy. Those who are affected by such reforms cannot complain that their property has been 325 taken from them, inasmuch as the only ground for their previous possession was the opinion of the people, which, as long as it remains unchanged, makes the possession necessarily valid. As soon as public opinion changes, however—but public opinion only as it is reflected in the judgment of those who through their merits have the best claim to lead it—then the presumptive ownership must cease just as though it had been lost through an appeal to the state (*a rege male informato ad regem melius informandum*).

This original acquired basic ownership provides the basis of the right of the chief magistrate as supreme proprietor (or lord of the country) to tax the private owners of land. This right permits him to levy land taxes, excises, and customs or services. Although this procedure will conform to laws of justice and right only when the people tax themselves through their corps of deputies, compulsory loans (deviating from the previously established law) may be imposed by the right of majesty in one situation, namely, when the state is in danger of being dissolved.

On this supreme proprietorship also rests the right of the supreme commander to administer the national economy, finances, and police. The police provide for public security, convenience, and decency. (It is important to provide for public decency, for if the feeling for decency (*sensus decori*)—considered as negative taste—is not benumbed by the prevalence of beggars, excessive street noises, offensive odors, and public prostitution, all of which violate the moral sensibilities, then the business of ruling the people through laws is made considerably easier for the government.)

There is still a third right that belongs to the state for its preservation: the right of inspection (*jus inspectionis*). By this right, no association (political or religious) that can have any influence on the public welfare of the society (*publicum*) may remain concealed, and such an association may not refuse to reveal its constitution if the police demand that it do so. However, the search of the private residence of anyone by the police is allowed only in case of necessity, and in every instance it must be authorized by a higher authority.

C [*Public Welfare: The Poor, Foundling Hospitals, Churches*]

Indirectly, inasmuch as he takes over the duty of the people, the supreme commander possesses the right to levy taxes on

them for their own conservation, in particular, for the relief of 326
the poor, foundling hospitals, and churches; in other words,
for what are usually called charitable and pious institutions.

The general Will of the people has united itself into a
society in order to maintain itself continually, and for this
purpose it has subjected itself to the internal authority of the
state in order to support those members of the society who
are not able to support themselves. Therefore, it follows from
the nature of the state that the government is authorized to
require the wealthy to provide the means of sustenance to
those who are unable to provide the most necessary needs of
nature for themselves. Because their existence depends on the
act of subjecting themselves to the commonwealth for the
protection and care required in order to stay alive, they have
bound themselves to contribute to the support of their fellow
citizens, and this is the ground for the state's right to require
them to do so. [In order to fulfill this function, the state may]
tax the property of the citizens or their commerce or establish
funds and use the interest from them; but the money cannot
be used for the needs of the state as such, since the state is
rich, but only for the needs of the people. The money should
not be raised merely through voluntary contributions, but by
compulsory exactions as political burdens, for here we are
considering only the rights of the state in relation to the
people. (Some voluntary contributions, such as lotteries, are
made for gain; but lotteries ought not to be permitted because
they increase the number of the poor and bring greater
dangers to public property than there would be without them.)
In this connection, we might ask whether the funds for the
care of the poor should be raised from current contributions
so that each generation will support its own poor or whether
it would be better to have recourse to permanent funds that
are collected gradually or to pious foundations in general
(such as widows' homes, hospitals, and so on). In any case, the
funds should not be raised by begging, which is closely related to robbery, but by lawful assessments. The first arrangement—current contributions—must be considered the only one

compatible with the rights of the state, which cannot abandon anyone who has to live; because, by using current contributions when the number of poor people increases, the profession of poverty will not become a means of livelihood for the lazy (as, it may be feared, is likely to happen in pious foundations), and thus the state will not be required to impose a [judicially] unjust burden on the people.

As for children abandoned because of poverty or out of shame or even murdered for these reasons, the state has the right to charge the people with the duty of not letting them perish knowingly, even though they are an unwelcome addition to the population. Whether this should be arranged by taxing the old bachelors and spinsters (that is, rich unmarried people)—who, as such, are in part responsible for the evil— for the purpose of establishing foundling hospitals or whether it can be done justly by some other means (other means of doing it justly might be difficult to find)—this is a problem that has not yet been solved without running into conflict either with right and justice or with morality.

[The state will also be concerned with the church, which fills one of its true needs.] At the very outset, we must carefully distinguish the church from religion, which is an inner attitude of mind quite outside the effective jurisdiction of civil power. The church, on the other hand, is an institution for public divine worship serving the people, to whose opinion or conviction it owes its origin. For the state, the church serves the need felt by the people to regard themselves as subjects of a highest unseen power to which they must pay homage and which can often come into unequal conflict with the civil power. Consequently, though the state does not have the right to order the internal constitutional legislation of the church for its own purposes or to prescribe or command the beliefs and rituals (*ritus*) of the people (for all this must be left entirely to the teachers and elders whom they have chosen for themselves), the state does have a negative right to prevent any activities of the public teachers that might prejudice the public peace. Thus, it may intervene in an internal controversy or in a controversy between churches in order to prevent any danger to civil harmony. This negative right is also a right of the police. Nevertheless, it is beneath the dignity of the supreme authority to meddle to the extent of determining that a church should hold one particular belief and which one it should have or that it should keep this belief unaltered and may not reform itself; for, by participating in a scholastic wrangle, he is placing himself on a footing of equality with his subjects (the monarch makes himself into a priest), and they can tell him bluntly that he does not understand such matters. All this applies especially to the prohibition by the supreme authority of any internal reforms, for what the whole people cannot decide concerning itself cannot be decided by the legislator for the people. But the people cannot now decide never to make any progress in their insights as regards their faith (in enlightenment), nor can they resolve never to reform their church, because to do so would conflict with the humanity in their own person and would be incompatible with the highest right of the people. It also follows that the supreme authority cannot make such a decision with regard to the people. As far as the cost of maintenance of the church is concerned, for the same reason the burden of paying does not devolve on the state, but must be borne by that segment of the people which adheres to this or that faith, in other words, the congregation.[10]

328

D [Public Offices—the Nobility]

The rights of the supreme commander also include: (1) the distribution of offices that involve employment for pay; (2) the distribution of positions of dignity [Würden] that are distinctions of rank not involving pay and that are based on honor alone; these distinctions of rank establish a superior class (entitled to command) and an inferior class (which, although free and bound only by public law, is predestined to obey the

[10] [See Appendix, § 8, pp. 133–137 below, for additional remarks on the subject of this section.]

former); (3) in addition to these (relatively beneficent) rights, the supreme commander has rights that concern the penal Law.

When we consider civil offices, the question arises: Does the sovereign have the right, after he has given an office to someone, to take it away again at his own discretion (without any crime having been committed by the holder of the office)? I say, "No," for the chief of state can never make a decision about a civil official that the united Will of the people would never make. Now, without any doubt, the people, who are supposed to bear the costs incurred by the appointment of an official, want such an official to be fully competent in the job assigned to him; but this is possible only after the person in question has spent a sufficiently long time in preparation and training, time which he could have spent in learning some other job in order to secure a means of livelihood. But, if arbitrary dismissals were permitted, then the civil service would be filled with people who would not have the requisite ability and mature judgment that is acquired through practical experience, and this would be contrary to the intentions of the state. Indeed, the state must make it possible for every individual to rise from a lower office to higher offices (which would otherwise fall into the hands of incompetents) and for every official to be able to count on a secure income for the rest of his life.

Under positions of dignity, we must include not only those attached to a political office, but also those that make the holders into members of a higher class or rank without performing any particular political services—in other words, the nobility as distinct from the class of common citizens who constitute the people. The rank of nobility is inherited by 329 male descendants and is also acquired by their wives who are not nobly born. However, a woman born to the nobility does not convey her rank to a husband not nobly born; instead, she herself returns to the class of common citizens (the people). The question that we must now ask is whether the sovereign is justified in establishing a nobility as a hereditary class between himself and the rest of the citizens of the state. In this question, we are not concerned with whether it would be expedient for the sovereign or to the advantage of the people to do so. Here we are interested only in whether it would be consistent with the rights of the people to have a class of persons above them who are, by reasons of their [noble] birth, commanders in relation to them or, at least, have certain privileges.

As before [in the case of the dismissal of officials], the answer to this question is to be derived from the principle: "What the people (the mass of subjects) cannot decide with regard to themselves or their fellows also cannot be decided by the sovereign regarding them." Now, a hereditary nobility is a class of persons who acquire their rank before they have merited it. Furthermore, there is no reason to hope that they will merit it. To think so is pure fancy and quite unrealistic, for, even if an ancestor had merit, he obviously could not bequeath it to his descendants, each of whom must earn it for himself; it is clear that nature has not arranged it so that the talent and [good] Will that are necessary for meritorious service to the state are hereditary. Inasmuch as it can be assumed that no man would throw away his freedom, it is impossible that the general Will of the people would consent to such a groundless prerogative, and therefore neither can the sovereign make it valid.

It may happen, however, that an anomaly such as subjects who want to be more than just citizens, that is, hereditary officials (imagine a hereditary professor!), have crept into the machinery of a government in ancient times (under feudalism, which was almost entirely organized for making war). Under such circumstances, the only course of action for the state to take in order to rectify this earlier mistake of unjustly [*widerrechtlich*] conferring hereditary privileges is to eliminate them gradually, either by agreement or by allowing the positions to become vacant. Consequently, the state provisionally has a right to allow these positions of dignity based on titles to continue until public opinion comes to recognize that the threefold division into sovereign, nobility, and people should be replaced by the only natural division, namely, sovereign and people.

No human being in the state can indeed be without any position of dignity at all, inasmuch as he has at least that dignity adhering to a citizen. The only exception is someone 330 who has lost it by his own criminal act, in which case, although he is allowed to stay alive, he is made into a mere tool of the will of someone else (either of the state or of another citizen). Such a person (and he can become one only through judgment and Law) is a slave (*servus in sensu stricto*) and is owned by someone else (*dominium*). The latter is, therefore, not merely his master (*herus*), but also his owner (*dominus*); being his owner, he can sell or alienate him as a thing, can use him as he pleases (but not for ignominious purposes), and can dispose of his abilities and energies [*Kräfte*], although not of his life or limbs.

No one can bind himself by a contract to the kind of dependency through which he ceases to be a person, for he can make a contract only insofar as he is a person. Now, it might seem that a person could obligate himself through a work contract (*locatio conductio*) to perform certain services (for wages, board, or protection), such that the services to be performed would be of the kind that is permissible, but would not be specified in amount; and it might be held that this would make him only a servant (*subjectus*) and not a slave (*servus*). Nevertheless, this is a mistake and an illusion, because, if a master is authorized to make use of the energies and abilities [*Kräfte*] of his servant as he pleases, he could utterly exhaust him and reduce him to death or despair (as has been done with the Negroes in the Sugar Islands); thus, in effect, the servant will have given himself away to his master to be owned by him, and this is impossible. It follows that someone can hire himself out only to do work that is specified both as to kind and amount, either as a day laborer or as a "live-in" servant. In the latter case, he might make a contract in part to labor on his master's land [in exchange] for the use

of it instead of drawing wages and in part to pay a certain
amount of rent [*Abgabe, Zins*] for his private utilization of
the same land; and all this would be specified in the lease.
This is possible without his making himself into a serf (*glebae
adscriptus*) and so losing his personality. Thus, he would still
be able to make a leasehold for a number of years or in perpetuity [*Zeit- oder Erbpacht*]. Even supposing that he has become a personal subject as the result of having committed a
crime, his servile status still cannot be transmitted to others
by inheritance, inasmuch as it is the penalty of his own guilt.
Much less can the offspring of such a slave be claimed as another slave on the ground that it cost so much to raise and
educate him; for parents have a natural duty to educate
their children, and, if the parents happen to be slaves, this
duty devolves on their masters, who take over the duties of
their slaves along with the possession of them.

E. The Penal Law and the Law of Pardon   331

I [*The Right to Punish*]

The right to punish contained in the penal law [*das Straf-
recht*] is the right that the magistrate has to inflict pain on
a subject in consequence of his having committed a crime.
It follows that the suzerain of the state cannot himself be
punished; we can only remove ourselves from his jurisdiction. A transgression of the public law that makes him who
commits it unfit to be a citizen is called either simply a crime
(*crimen*) or a public crime (*crimen publicum*). [If, however,
we call it a public crime, then we can use the term "crime"
generically to include both private and public crimes.] [11] The
first (a private crime) is brought before a civil court, and the
second (a public crime), before a criminal court. Embezzle-
ment, that is, misappropriation of money or wares entrusted

[11] [Natorp and Cassirer agree that there is something wrong with the
sentence following this one. Either a sentence has been omitted or the
sentence in question has been misplaced. Kant's meaning is, however, perfectly clear, and I have inserted a sentence to provide the transition.]

in commerce, and fraud in buying and selling, if perpetrated before the eyes of the party who suffers, are private crimes. On the other hand, counterfeiting money or bills of exchange, theft, robbery, and similar acts are public crimes, because through them the commonwealth and not just a single individual is exposed to danger. These crimes may be divided into those of a base character (*indolis abjectae*) and those of a violent character (*indolis violentae*).

Judicial punishment (*poena forensis*) is entirely distinct from natural punishment (*poena naturalis*). In natural punishment, vice punishes itself, and this fact is not taken into consideration by the legislator. Judicial punishment can never be used merely as a means to promote some other good for the criminal himself or for civil society, but instead it must in all cases be imposed on him only on the ground that he has committed a crime; for a human being can never be manipulated merely as a means to the purposes of someone else and can never be confused with the objects of the Law of things [*Sachenrecht*]. His innate personality [that is, his right as a person] protects him against such treatment, even though he may indeed be condemned to lose his civil personality. He must first be found to be deserving of punishment before any consideration is given to the utility of this punishment for himself or for his fellow citizens. The law concerning punishment is a categorical imperative, and woe to him who rummages around in the winding paths of a theory of happiness looking for some advantage to be gained by releasing the criminal from punishment or by reducing the amount of it—in keeping with the Pharisaic motto: "It is better that one man should die than that the whole people should perish." If legal justice perishes, then it is no longer worth while for men to remain alive on this earth. If this is so, what should one think of the proposal to permit a criminal who has been condemned to death to remain alive, if, after consenting to allow dangerous experiments to be made on him, he happily survives such experiments and if doctors thereby obtain new information that benefits the community? Any court of justice would repudiate such a proposal with scorn if it were suggested by a medical college, for [legal] justice ceases to be justice if it can be bought for a price.

What kind and what degree of punishment does public legal justice adopt as its principle and standard? None other than the principle of equality (illustrated by the pointer on the scales of justice), that is, the principle of not treating one side more favorably than the other. Accordingly, any undeserved evil that you inflict on someone else among the people is one that you do to yourself. If you vilify him, you vilify yourself; if you steal from him, you steal from yourself; if you kill him, you kill yourself. Only the Law of retribution (*jus talionis*) can determine exactly the kind and degree of punishment; it must be well understood, however, that this determination [must be made] in the chambers of a court of justice (and not in your private judgment). All other standards fluctuate back and forth and, because extraneous considerations are mixed with them, they cannot be compatible with the principle of pure and strict legal justice.

Now, it might seem that the existence of class distinctions would not allow for the [application of the] retributive principle of returning like for like. Nevertheless, even though these class distinctions may not make it possible to apply this principle to the letter, it can still always remain applicable in its effects if regard is had to the special sensibilities of the higher classes. Thus, for example, the imposition of a fine for a verbal injury has no proportionality to the original injury, for someone who has a good deal of money can easily afford to make insults whenever he wishes. On the other hand, the humiliation of the pride of such an offender comes much closer to equaling an injury done to the honor of the person offended; thus the judgment and Law might require the offender, not only to make a public apology to the offended person, but also at the same time to kiss his hand, even though he be socially inferior. Similarly, if a man of a higher class has violently attacked an innocent citizen who is socially inferior to him, he may be condemned, not only to apologize, but to undergo soli-

333 tary and painful confinement, because by this means, in addition to the discomfort suffered, the pride of the offender will be painfully affected, and thus his humiliation will compensate for the offense as like for like.

But what is meant by the statement: "If you steal from him, you steal from yourself"? Inasmuch as someone steals, he makes the ownership of everyone else insecure, and hence he robs himself (in accordance with the Law of retribution) of the security of any possible ownership. He has nothing and can also acquire nothing, but he still wants to live, and this is not possible unless others provide him with nourishment. But, because the state will not support him gratis, he must let the state have his labor at any kind of work it may wish to use him for (convict labor), and so he becomes a slave, either for a certain period of time or indefinitely, as the case may be.

If, however, he has committed a murder, he must die. In this case, there is no substitute that will satisfy the requirements of legal justice. There is no sameness of kind between death and remaining alive even under the most miserable conditions, and consequently there is also no equality between the crime and the retribution unless the criminal is judicially condemned and put to death. But the death of the criminal must be kept entirely free of any maltreatment that would make an abomination of the humanity residing in the person suffering it. Even if a civil society were to dissolve itself by common agreement of all its members (for example, if the people inhabiting an island decided to separate and disperse themselves around the world), the last murderer remaining in prison must first be executed, so that everyone will duly receive what his actions are worth and so that the bloodguilt thereof will not be fixed on the people because they failed to insist on carrying out the punishment; for if they fail to do so, they may be regarded as accomplices in this public violation of legal justice.

Furthermore, it is possible for punishment to be equal in accordance with the strict Law of retribution only if the judge pronounces the death sentence. This is clear because only in this way will the death sentence be pronounced on all criminals in proportion to their inner viciousness (even if the crime involved is not murder, but some other crime against the state that can be expiated only by death). To illustrate this point, let us consider a situation, like the last Scottish rebellion, in which the participants are motivated by varying purposes, just as in that rebellion some believed that they were only fulfilling their obligations to the house of Stuart (like Balmerino and others),[12] and others, in contrast, were pursuing their own private interests. Suppose that the highest court were to pronounce as follows: Each person shall have the freedom to choose between death and penal servitude. I say that a man of honor would choose death and that the knave would choose servitude. This is implied by the nature of human character, because the first recognizes something that he prizes more highly than life itself, namely, honor, whereas the second thinks that a life covered with disgrace is still better than not being alive at all (*animam praeferre pudori*).[13] The first is without doubt less deserving of punishment than the other, and so, if they are both condemned to die, they will be punished exactly in proportion [to their inner viciousness]; the first will be punished mildly in terms of his kind of sensibility, and the second will be punished severely in terms of his kind of sensibility. On the other hand, if both were condemned to penal servitude, the first would be punished too severely and

334

12 [Arthur Elphinstone, Sixth Baron Balmerino (1688–1746), participated in the Jacobite rebellion that attempted to put Prince Charles Edward Stuart on the British throne. He was captured, tried, found guilty, and beheaded. He is said to have acted throughout with great constancy and courage.]

13 ["To prefer life to honor"—Juvenal, *Satire* 8. 83. The complete text, lines 79–84, is quoted by Kant in the *Critique of Practical Reason*, Part II: "Be a stout soldier, a faithful guardian, and an incorruptible judge; if summoned to bear witness in some dubious and uncertain cause, though Phalaris himself should command you to tell lies and bring up his bull and dictate to you a perjury, count it the greatest of all sins to prefer life to honour, and to lose, for the sake of living, all that makes life worth having." Trans. G. G. Ramsey, "Loeb Classical Library." (Phalaris, tyrant of Agrigentum, had criminals burned to death in a brass ox.)]

the second too mildly for their baseness. Thus, even in sentences imposed on a number of criminals united in a plot, the best equalizer before the bar of public legal justice is death.

It may also be pointed out that no one has ever heard of anyone condemned to death on account of murder who complained that he was getting too much [punishment] and therefore was being treated unjustly; everyone would laugh in his face if he were to make such a statement. Indeed, otherwise we would have to assume that, although the treatment accorded the criminal is not unjust according to the law, the legislative authority still is not authorized to decree this kind of punishment and that, if it does so, it comes into contradiction with itself.

Anyone who is a murderer—that is, has committed a murder, commanded one, or taken part in one—must suffer death. This is what [legal] justice as the Idea of the judicial authority wills in accordance with universal laws that are grounded a priori. The number of accomplices (*correi*) in such a deed might, however, be so large that the state would soon approach the condition of having no more subjects if it were to rid itself of these criminals, and this would lead to its dissolution and a return to the state of nature, which is much worse, because it would be a state of affairs without any external legal justice whatsoever. Since a sovereign will want to avoid such consequences and, above all, will want to avoid adversely affecting the feelings of the people by the spectacle of such butchery, he must have it within his power in case of necessity (*casus necessitatis*) to assume the role of judge and to pronounce a judgment that, instead of imposing the death penalty on the criminals, assigns some other punishment that will make the preservation of the mass of the people possible, such as, for example, deportation. Such a course of action would not come under a public law, but would be an executive decree [*Machtspruch*], that is, an act based on the right of majesty, which, as an act of reprieve, can be exercised only in individual cases.

In opposition to this view, the Marquis of Beccaria,[14] moved

14 [Cesare Bonesana, Marquis di Beccaria (1738–1794), Italian publicist. His *Dei delitti e delle pene* (1764) (*On Crimes and Punishments*, trans.

by sympathetic sentimentality and an affectation of humanitarianism, has asserted that all capital punishment is illegitimate. He argues that it could not be contained in the original civil contract, inasmuch as this would imply that every one of the people has agreed to forfeit his life if he murders another (of the people); but such an agreement would be impossible, for no one can dispose of his own life.

No one suffers punishment because he has willed the punishment, but because he has willed a punishable action. If what happens to someone is also willed by him, it cannot be a punishment. Accordingly, it is impossible to will to be punished. To say, "I will to be punished if I murder someone," can mean nothing more than, "I submit myself along with everyone else to those laws which, if there are any criminals among the people, will naturally include penal laws." In my role as colegislator making the penal law, I cannot be the same person who, as subject, is punished by the law; for, as a subject who is also a criminal, I cannot have a voice in legislation. (The legislator is holy.) When, therefore, I enact a penal law against myself as a criminal it is the pure juridical legislative reason (*homo noumenon*) in me that submits myself to the penal law as a person capable of committing a crime, that is, as another person (*homo phaenomenon*) along with all the others in the civil union who submit themselves to this law. In other words, it is not the people (considered as individuals) who dictate the death penalty, but the court (public legal justice); that is, someone other than the criminal. The social contract does not include the promise to permit oneself to be punished and thus to dispose of oneself and of one's life, because, if the only ground that authorizes the punishment of an evildoer were a promise that expresses his willingness to be punished, then it would have to be left up to him to find himself liable to punishment, and the criminal would be his own judge. The chief error contained in this sophistry (πρωτον ψευδος) consists in the confusion of the criminal's own judg-

Henry Paolucci, "The Library of Liberal Arts," No. 107 [New York: The Liberal Arts Press, 1963]) was widely read and had great influence on the reform of the penal codes of various European states.]

ment (which one must necessarily attribute to his reason) that he must forfeit his life with a resolution of the Will to take his own life. The result is that the execution of the Law and the adjudication thereof are represented as united in the same person.

There remain, however, two crimes deserving of death with regard to which it still remains doubtful whether legislation is authorized to impose the death penalty. In both cases, the crimes are due to the sense of honor. One involves the honor of womanhood; the other, military honor. Both kinds of honor are genuine, and duty requires that they be sought after by every individual in each of these two classes. The first crime is infanticide at the hands of the mother (*infanticidium maternale*); the other is the murder of a fellow soldier (*commilitonicidium*) in a duel.

Now, legislation cannot take away the disgrace of an illegitimate child, nor can it wipe away the stain of suspicion of cowardice from a junior officer who fails to react to a humiliating affront with action that would show that he has the strength to overcome the fear of death. Accordingly, it seems that, in such circumstances, the individuals concerned find themselves in a state of nature, in which killing another (*homicidium*) can never be called murder (*homicidium dolosum*); in both cases, they are indeed deserving of punishment, but they cannot be punished with death by the supreme power. A child born into the world outside marriage is outside the law (for this is [implied by the concept of] marriage), and consequently it is also outside the protection of the law. The child has crept surreptitiously into the commonwealth (much like prohibited wares), so that its existence as well as its destruction can be ignored (because by right it ought not to have come into existence in this way); and the mother's disgrace if the illegitimate birth becomes known cannot be wiped out by any official decree.

Similarly, a military man who has been commissioned a junior officer may suffer an insult and as a result feel obliged by the opinions of his comrades in arms to seek satisfaction and to punish the person who insulted him, not by appealing

336

to the law and taking him to court, but instead, as would be done in a state of nature, by challenging him to a duel; for, even though in doing so he will be risking his life, he will thereby be able to demonstrate his military valor, on which the honor of his profession rests. If, under such circumstances, his opponent should be killed, this cannot properly be called a murder (*homicidium dolosum*), inasmuch as it takes place in a combat openly fought with the consent of both parties, even though they may have participated in it only reluctantly.

What, then, is the actual Law of the land with regard to these two cases (which come under criminal justice)? This question presents penal justice with a dilemma: either it must declare that the concept of honor (which is no delusion in these cases) is null and void in the eyes of the law and that these acts should be punished by death or it must abstain from imposing the death penalty for these crimes, which merit it; thus it must be either too cruel or too lenient. The solution to this dilemma is as follows: the categorical imperative involved in the legal justice of punishment remains valid (that is, the unlawful killing of another person must be punished 337 by death), but legislation itself (including also the civil constitution), as long as it remains barbaric and undeveloped, is responsible for the fact that incentives of honor among the people do not accord (subjectively) with the standards that are (objectively) appropriate to their purpose, with the result that public legal justice as administered by the state is injustice from the point of view of the people.[15]

II [*The Right to Pardon*]

The right to pardon a criminal (*jus aggratiandi*), either by mitigating or by entirely remitting the punishment, is cer-

[15] [See Appendix, § 5. In the *Critique of Pure Reason*, trans. Kemp Smith, B 373, Kant writes: "The more legislation and government are brought into harmony with the . . . idea . . . (of a constitution allowing *the greatest possible human freedom* in accordance with laws by which *the freedom of each is made to be consistent with that of all others*) . . . the rarer would punishments become, and it is therefore quite rational to maintain, as Plato does, that in a perfect state no punishments whatsoever would be required." The order of the sentence has been changed.]

tainly the most slippery of all the rights of the sovereign. By exercising it he can demonstrate the splendor of his majesty and yet thereby wreak injustice [*unrecht*] to a high degree. With respect to a crime of one subject against another, he absolutely cannot exercise this right, for in such cases exemption from punishment (*impunitas criminis*) constitutes the greatest injustice toward his subjects. Consequently, he can make use of this right of pardon only in connection with an injury committed against himself (*crimen laesae majestatis*). But, even in these cases, he cannot allow a crime to go unpunished if the safety of the people might be endangered thereby. The right to pardon is the only one that deserves the name of a "right of majesty."

§ 50 [THE JURIDICAL RELATIONSHIPS OF A CITIZEN TO HIS OWN AND TO FOREIGN COUNTRIES]

A territory whose inhabitants are already citizens of the same commonwealth by virtue of the constitution, that is to say, without having to execute any special juridical act (and are consequently citizens by birth), is called their country [or fatherland]. A territory in which they are not citizens unless such special conditions are fulfilled is called a foreign country [*das Ausland*]; and, when a country is under the general dominion of a government, it is called a province (in the sense in which the Romans used this word). A province must respect the land of the ruling state as the "mother country" (*regio domina*), since it is not incorporated as part of the realm as such (*imperii*), wherein the fellow citizens reside, but is only a possession of the realm, to which it is subject.

338   (1) A subject (regarded also as citizen) has the right to emigrate, for the state cannot detain him as a piece of property. Nevertheless, he can take only his movable belongings and not his fixed belongings with him out of the country; the latter would take place if he were authorized to sell the land that he possessed and to take with him the money that he received for it.

(2) The lord of a country [*Landesherr*] has the right to encourage foreigners (colonists) to immigrate and settle in his country, even though his native subjects do not regard this action favorably. He may do so, however, only providing that the private ownership of the land of the natives is not diminished.

(3) In the case of a subject who has committed a crime that makes association with his fellow citizens dangerous to the state, the lord of the country has the right to banish him to a province outside the country, where he will no longer participate in any of the rights of a citizen; that is, he may deport him.

(4) He even has the right to exile such a criminal from his domain altogether (*jus exilii*) and to send him out into the world at large, that is, outside his country altogether [*das Ausland überhaupt*] (which is called *Elend* ["misery"] in Old German). Since the lord of the country thereby withdraws his protection, this action amounts to making him an outlaw within the boundaries of his own country.

§ 51 [THE THREE FORMS OF THE STATE: AUTOCRACY, ARISTOCRACY, AND DEMOCRACY]

The three authorities in the state that proceed out of the concept of a commonwealth in general (*res publica latius dicta*) are nothing more than so many relationships in the united Will of the people, which originates a priori in reason. They constitute the pure Idea of a chief of state, and this Idea possesses objective practical reality. This chief (the sovereign) is, however, only an abstract object of thought (representing the whole people) as long as there is no physical person to represent the highest authority of the state and to procure an effective influence of this Idea on the popular Will. The relationship of the highest authority in the state to the people may be conceived in three ways: a single person in the state has command over all, or several persons who are equal and united have command over all the rest, or all the people together have command over each person, including themselves. Accordingly, the form of the state may be autocratic, aristocratic, or democratic. (It would be improper to use the term "monarchical" instead of "autocratic" for the concept intended here, for a monarch is one who possesses only the highest authority, whereas an autocrat, or "self-commander," is one who possesses all the authority. The latter is the sovereign; the former merely represents him.)

It can be easily seen that the autocratic form of the state is the simplest [because it contains only one relationship], namely, that of a single person (the king) to the people, and consequently there is only one legislator in an autocracy. The aristocratic form of the state is already composed of two relationships, namely, the relationship of the nobles (as legislators) to one another that constitutes them a sovereign and the relationship of this sovereign to the people. The democratic form of the state is the most complex [for it contains the following relationships]: first, the Will of all to unite to constitute themselves a people; then, the Will of the citizens to form a commonwealth; and, finally, [their Will] to place at the head of this commonwealth a sovereign, who is none other than this united Will itself.[16] As far as the administration of justice in the state is concerned, the simplest form is without doubt also at the same time the best; but, as far as justice and Law are concerned, the simplest form is the most dangerous for the people in view of the fact that it strongly invites despotism. Simplification is indeed a reasonable maxim in the machinery of uniting the people through coercive laws, provided that all the people are passive and obey the one person who is above them; but, under such circumstances, none of the subjects are citizens. [Under such a government,] the people are supposed to remain content with the hope that is held out to them that monarchy (more correctly, autocracy) is the best political con-

16 I shall not discuss here the perversion of these forms that arises from the usurpation of power by unauthorized persons (oligarchy and ochlocracy) or so-called mixed political constitutions, for to do so would lead us too far afield.

stitution as long as the *monarch is good* (not only has a good Will, but also the requisite intelligence). But this statement is just a tautological wise saying inasmuch as it says no more than that the best constitution is one that makes the administrator into the best ruler; in other words, it is that which is the best!

§ 52 [THE IDEAL STATE]

To inquire after the historical origin of this mechanism of government is futile; that is to say, it is impossible to reach back to the time at which the civil society came into being (for savages do not draw up documents when they submit themselves to the law, and, indeed, from the very nature of uncivilized men it can be inferred that this [original submission] was achieved through the use of violence). It would, however, be a crime to conduct such an inquiry with the intention of [finding a pretext] for changing the present existing constitu-   340 tion by force. This kind of transformation [of the constitution] could only be effected by the people acting as a riotous mob, not by means of legislation; and insurrection under an existing constitution involves the destruction of all civil juridical relationships, including all Law. Thus it is not an alteration of the civil constitution, but the dissolution of it; and the transition to a better constitution is not a metamorphosis, but a palingenesis. This in turn requires a new civil contract, on which the former contract (which is now null and void) has no influence.

Nevertheless, it must still be possible for the sovereign to change the existing constitution if it does not accord well with the Idea of the original contract and by this means to introduce that form that is essential in order for the people to constitute a state. This change cannot be such that the state transforms itself from one of these three forms to another, for example, by an agreement among the aristocrats to submit to an autocracy or to convert to a democracy or conversely; for, in doing so, the sovereign would be acting as though it were a matter of his own free choice and pleasure to decide to which kind of constitution he wants the people to submit. Even if the sovereign were to decide to transform himself into a democracy, he would still be doing the people an injustice, because the people themselves might abhor this kind of constitution and might find that one of the other two was more advantageous for them.

The forms of the state are, as it were, only the *letter* (*littera*) [17] of the original legislation in civil society, and they may therefore continue as long as they are held by ancient, long-standing custom (hence only subjectively) to be necessary to the machinery of the constitution of the state. However, the *spirit* of that original contract (*anima pacti originarii*) entails the obligation of the constituted authority to make the type of government conform to this Idea and, accordingly, to change the government gradually and continually, if it cannot be done at one time, so that it will effectively agree with the one and only legitimate constitution, namely, that of a pure republic. Thus, those old (statutory) empirical forms of the state, which serve only to effect the subjection of the people, must be transmuted into the original (rational) form, which is the only one that makes freedom its principle and, indeed, the condition of every use of coercion. Coercion under the condition of freedom is required for a juridical constitution of the state in the proper and true sense, and, when this has been accomplished, the spirit of the constitution will also have become the letter [that is, actual law].[18]

341   This [republican] constitution is the only enduring political constitution in which the law is autonomous [*selbstherrschend*] and is not annexed to any particular person. It is the ultimate end of all public Law and the only condition under

17 [Kant is here making a distinction between the letter (*Buchstabe*) and the spirit (*Geist*) of the law or constitution. The distinction that Kant has in mind is probably the same as that made in modern jurisprudence between "the law as it is" and "the law as it ought to be."]

18 [The construction of the last part of this sentence is not entirely clear, so I have translated it rather freely to accord with what has gone before.]

which each person receives his due peremptorily; for, as long as, according to the letter [that is, in actuality], the other forms of the state represent so many distinct moral persons as invested with the supreme authority, it must be recognized that only a provisory internal justice and no absolutely juridical state of civil society can exist.

Every true republic is and can be nothing else than a representative system of the people if it is to protect the rights of its citizens in the name of the people. Under a representative system, these rights are protected by the citizens themselves, united and acting through their representatives (deputies). As soon, however, as the chief of state in person (whether it be a king, the nobility, or the whole population—the democratic union) also allows himself to be represented, then the united people do not merely represent the sovereign, but they themselves *are* the sovereign. The supreme authority resided originally in the people, and all the rights of individuals considered as mere subjects (and especially as political officials) must be derived from this supreme authority. Accordingly, the republic that has now been instituted no longer needs to let the reins of government out of its hands and to return them to those who had them previously, to those who could then by their absolute and arbitrary will destroy the new institutions again.

Thus, a great error in judgment was made by one of the powerful sovereigns of our time when he attempted to extricate himself from the embarrassment caused by large state debts by leaving it to the people to take over this burden and to distribute it as they saw fit.[19] The natural result was that he handed over to the people legislative authority, not only over taxation, but also over the gov-

19 [Kant is referring to the revolutionary constitutional developments in France after the calling of the Estates General, May 5, 1789, by Louis XVI in order to extricate himself from financial difficulties. This body first transformed itself into the National Assembly and then, as the Constituent Assembly, adopted a new constitution on September 3, 1791, that reduced the monarchy to impotence. Later, the monarchy was eliminated entirely.]

ernment, that is, authority to restrain the government
from making new debts through the extravagance of war.
As a consequence, the sovereignty of the monarch disappeared completely (it was not just suspended) and passed
over to the people, to whose legislative Will the property
of every subject now became subject. Nor can it be contended that in this case we have to assume that the national assembly made a tacit (contractual) promise not to
342 make itself the sovereign, but just to administer the business for the sovereign and promised to relinquish the
reins of government into the hands of the monarch after
it finished this business. It is impossible to make such an
assumption, because a contract of this kind would be null
and void inasmuch as the right of supreme legislation in
a commonwealth is not an alienable right, but the most
personal of all rights. Whoever possesses this right can
control and direct the people [*disponieren*] through the
collective Will of the people, but cannot dispose of the
collective Will itself, for the collective Will itself is the
first and original foundation of any public contract whatsoever. A contract that would obligate the people to give
back its authority could not be consistent with its role as
legislative power, and to hold that such a contract has
any binding force is self-contradictory by the principle:
"No man can serve two masters."

second section
THE LAW OF NATIONS
343
§ 53 [DEFINITION OF THE LAW OF NATIONS]

Those individual human beings who make up a nation [1]
can, as natives of the country, be represented as the offspring

1 [The German *Volk* can be translated by either "people" or "nation."
In general, I shall use "nation" when the relations among nations are
involved and "people" where the internal relations among the people and
the state and its officials are involved. The reader should be warned, however, against attributing connotations of "nationalism" to Kant's use of
Volk.]

of a common ancestry (*congeniti*), although this is, of course, only a kind of analogy and is not strictly true. If, however, we interpret this relationship in an intellectual and juridical sense, a nation bears a resemblance to a family (*gens, natio*) whose members (citizens) are by birth equal to one another, having been born of a common mother (the republic). As such, they regard those who might happen to live next to them in a state of nature as social inferiors and consequently will not mingle or marry with them, even though the latter (the savages) think that they themselves are superior by virtue of the lawless freedom that they have chosen. People who live thus in a state of nature constitute primitive societies [*Völkerschaften*], rather than states.

Our present concern, however, is with the Law governing the relations among states [rather than among peoples or societies], although it has been given the name of the Law of nations [*Völkerrecht*]. (The expression "the Law of nations" is therefore a misnomer, and the Law concerned should more properly be called "the Law of states"—*jus publicum civitatum*.)

Under the Law of nations, a state is regarded as a moral person living with and in opposition to another state in a condition of natural freedom, which itself is a condition of continual war. [Accordingly, the Law of nations is concerned with those rights of a state that involve war in one way or another. These rights consist] partly of the right to make war, partly of rights during a war, and partly of rights after a war, namely, the right to compel each other to abandon the state of war and to establish a constitution that will guarantee an enduring peace. The principal difference between the state of nature that exists among individuals or families (in their relationship to one another) and that which exists among nations as such is that the Law of nations is concerned, not only with the relationship of one state to another, but also with relationships of individuals in one state to individuals in another and of an individual to another whole state. But this difference between the Law of nations and the Law of individuals in a state of

344

nature does not imply any [special] qualifications that are not easily deducible from the concept of the latter.

§ 54 [THE ELEMENTS OF THE LAW OF NATIONS]

The elements of the Law of nations are as follows:

(1) With regard to their external relationship to one another, states are naturally in a nonjuridical condition (like lawless savages).

(2) This condition is a state of war (the right of the stronger), even though there may not be an actual war or continuous fighting (hostility). Nevertheless (inasmuch as neither side wants to have it better), it is still a condition that is in the highest degree unjust, and it is a condition that states adjoining one another are obligated to abandon.

(3) A league of nations in accordance with the Idea of an original social contract is necessary, not, indeed, in order to meddle in one another's internal dissensions, but in order to afford protection against external aggression.

(4) But this alliance must not involve a sovereign authority (as in a civil constitution), but only a confederation. Such an alliance can be renounced at any time and therefore must be renewed from time to time. This is a right that follows as a corollary *in subsidium* from another right, which is original, namely, the right to protect oneself against the danger of becoming involved in an actual war among the adherents of the confederation (*foedus Amphictyonum*).[2]

§ 55 [THE RIGHT OF GOING TO WAR IN RELATION TO THE STATE'S OWN SUBJECTS]

In connection with the original right of free states in a state of nature to wage war against one another (in order perhaps to establish a condition closer to the juridical state

2 [An amphictyonic league was a league of neighboring states or tribes in ancient Greece that was formed for religious purposes and mutual protection. The most famous of these was the Theban amphictyony (sixth century B.C.).]

of affairs), the first question that arises is: What right does the state have over its own subjects in the war? May it employ them in the war, use their goods, or even expend their lives, regardless of their personal judgment as to whether they want to go to war? May the sovereign send them into the war through his supreme command [alone]?

It might seem that his right to do so could be easily demonstrated from the right that a person has to do whatever he wants to do with what belongs to him, that is, with what he owns. But everyone indisputably owns whatever he himself has substantially made [*der Substanz nach,* that is, something that he has actually brought into existence and has not merely changed]. This is the Deduction of this right as it would be formulated by a mere jurist. [Let us now examine the argument in more detail.]

In any country, there are, of course, various products of nature that nevertheless, because of their abundance, must be regarded as artifacts (*artefacta*) of the state, inasmuch as the land would not have produced so much had there been no state or powerful government, but the inhabitants had, instead, remained in a state of nature. For example, because of shortage of feed or beasts of prey, hens (the most useful species of bird), sheep, swine, cattle, and the like would either not exist at all in the country in which I live or would be exceedingly rare if there were no government to safeguard the acquisitions and possessions of its inhabitants. The same is true of the number of people [in a country], for [without a government] it can only remain small, just as it is in the American wilderness; indeed, the people would still remain small in numbers even if we were to assume that they are much more industrious [than those who live under a government] (as, of course, they are not). The inhabitants of such a country would be very sparse, since they would be unable to spread themselves out on the land with their households, because of the danger of devastation by other men, by savages, or by beasts of prey. Consequently, under such circumstances, there would be no adequate means of livelihood for such a great number

345

of people as now populate a country. Inasmuch as crops (for example, potatoes) and domestic animals are products of human labor, at least as far as their quantity is concerned, we can say that they may be used, consumed, or destroyed (killed). In the same vein, it might seem that we could say that the supreme authority in the state, the sovereign, also has the right to lead his subjects into a war as though it were a hunting expedition and to march them onto a field of battle as though it were a pleasure excursion on the grounds that they are for the most part products of his own activity.

This kind of argument for a right (which in all likelihood hovers darkly in the minds of monarchs) is indeed valid with respect to animals, which can be owned by human beings, but it absolutely cannot be applied to a human being, and especially not to a citizen. A citizen must always be regarded as a colegislative member of the state (that is, not merely as a means, but at the same time as an end in itself), and as such he must give his free consent through his representatives, not only to the waging of war in general, but also to any particular declaration of war. It is only under this limiting condition that the state may demand and dispose of a citizen's services if they involve being exposed to danger.

Therefore, we shall have to derive the right in question from the duty of the sovereign to the people (rather than conversely). [Moreover, if this right is exercised,] we must be certain that the people have given their consent, and, in this respect, even though they may be passive (in the sense that they merely comply), they are also still active autonomously and themselves represent the sovereign.

§ 56 [THE RIGHT OF GOING TO WAR IN RELATION TO OTHER STATES]

In the state of nature among states, the right to go to war (to commence hostilities) constitutes the permitted means by which one state prosecutes its right against another. In other words, a state is permitted to employ violent measures to secure redress when it believes that it has been injured by

another state, inasmuch as, in the state of nature, this cannot
be accomplished through a judicial process (which is the only
means by which such disputes are settled under a juridical
condition of affairs). [The offenses for which remedy may be
sought in this way include,] not only actual injury (through
first aggression, which is to be distinguished from first hostilities), but also threats. We may consider a threat to exist if
another state engages in military preparations, and this is the
basis of the right of preventive war (*jus praeventionis*). Or
even the mere menacing increase of power (*potentia tre-
menda*) of another state (through the acquisition of new territory) can be regarded as a threat, inasmuch as the mere
existence of a superior power is itself injurious to a lesser
power, and this makes an attack on the former undoubtedly
legitimate in a state of nature. On this is founded the right
to preserve a balance of power among all states that are con-
tiguous to one another and act on one another.

Among those overt attacks that provide grounds for the
exercise of the right to go to war, acts of retaliation (*retorsio*)
must be included, that is, acts by which one nation seeks
through self-help to gain redress for an injury done to it without attempting to obtain compensation (through peaceful
means). In its form, this procedure is much like starting a war
without declaring war beforehand. If, however, one wants to
find any justice or rights in a state of war, then something
analogous to a contract must be presupposed, namely, the acceptance of the declaration of war by the other party, so that
it can be assumed that both parties wish to pursue their rights
in this fashion.

§ 57 [RIGHTS DURING A WAR]

The question of justice and rights during a war presents
the greatest difficulty, inasmuch as it is difficult without con-
tradicting oneself even to form any concept of such a right
and to think of there being any law in a condition that is itself lawless (*inter arma silent leges*). If there is any justice and
right under such circumstances, it must be as follows: The war

must be conducted according to such principles as will not preclude the possibility of abandoning the state of nature existing among states (in their external relations) and of entering into a juridical condition.

No war between independent states can be a punitive one (*bellum punitivum*), for punishment takes place only where there is a relationship of a superior (*imperantis*) to a subject (*subditum*), and no such relationship exists between states. Nor can any war be one of extermination (*bellum internecinum*) or a war of subjugation (*bellum subjugatorium*), inasmuch as such wars result in the elimination of a state as a moral being by absorbing its people into one mass with the people of the conqueror or by reducing them to slavery. It is not that the state's use of such measures, if they were necessary to achieve peace, would in themselves contradict the rights of a state, but the Idea of the Law of nations only involves the concept of an antagonism that is in accordance with the principles of external freedom, that is to say, it permits the use of force only to maintain and preserve one's property and not as a means of acquisition of the kind that would result in the aggrandizement of one state becoming a threat to another.

To a state against which a war is being fought, defensive measures of every kind except those that would make a subject of that state unfit to be a citizen are allowed. If it were to employ such measures, it would thereby make itself unfit to be considered a person in relation to other states in the eyes of the Law of nations (and as such to participate in equal rights with the other states). Among such forbidden measures are the following: employing its subjects as spies and using them, or even foreigners, as assassins or poisoners (we should also include here so-called guerrillas [*Scharfschützen*], who wait for individuals in ambush) or just using them to spread false rumors; in a word, it is forbidden to employ any such treacherous measures as would destroy the mutual faith that is required if any enduring peace is to be established in the future.

During a war, although it is permissible to impose exactions and contributions on a vanquished enemy, it is still not 348
permissible to plunder the people, that is, to seize forcibly the
belongings of individuals (because that would be robbery, inasmuch as it was not the conquered people themselves who
waged the war, but the state to which they were subject and
which waged the war through them). Furthermore, receipts
should be given for any requisitions that are made, so that in
the peace that follows the burden that was imposed on the
country or province can be equitably distributed.

§ 58 [RIGHTS AFTER A WAR]

Justice and rights after a war, that is, at the time the peace
treaty is concluded and in relation to the consequences of the
treaty, consist in the following: The victor lays down the conditions, and these are customarily drawn up in a peace treaty,
to which the vanquished power is supposed to agree and
which leads to the conclusion of the peace. In laying down
these conditions, the victor makes no pretense of appealing
to a right against his opponent that is based on some supposed
injury from him, but, leaving such questions unanswered, he
rests his case on his strength [Gewalt] alone. It follows that the
conqueror cannot request compensation for the costs of the
war, inasmuch as, in doing so, he would have to admit that
the waging of war on the part of his opponent was unjust
[ungerecht]. Even if he thinks that this is a good argument,
he still cannot use it here, because, in doing so, he would be
declaring that the war was a punitive one, and, in waging a
punitive war, he himself would in turn be committing an
offense against his opponent. [On the conclusion of peace,]
there should be an exchange (with no ransom) of prisoners of
war without regard to the equality of the numbers of prisoners
released by each side.

Neither a conquered state nor its citizens lose their civil
freedom as a result of the capture of their country in the sense
that the former is degraded to the status of a colony or the
latter to that of slaves. It could be otherwise only if the war

had been a punitive one, which is self-contradictory. A colony or province consists of a people who, indeed, have their own constitution, legislation, and land. In this land, those people who belong to another state are aliens, even if their state has executive authority over the people in the colony or province. Such a state is called the "mother state." The "daughter state" is subject to the "mother state," but it rules itself (through its own parliament, which is usually presided over by a viceroy [*civitas hybrida*]). Such a relation existed between Athens and the various islands and now exists between Great Britain and Ireland.

349   It is even less possible to base slavery on the conquest of a people through war and to derive its legitimacy from this fact, for this would require us to assume that the war was a punitive one. Least of all would hereditary slavery based on conquest be possible; indeed, it would be quite absurd, inasmuch as the guilt from a person's crime cannot be inherited.

That a general amnesty should be included in a peace treaty is already implied in the concept of the latter.

§ 59 [THE RIGHTS OF PEACE]

The rights of peace are as follows: (1) the right to remain at peace when there is a war in the vicinity, that is, the right of neutrality; (2) the right to secure for oneself the continuation of a peace that has been concluded, that is, the right of guarantee; (3) the right to form reciprocal alliances with other states (confederations) for common defense against any possible attacks from without or from within; but this does not include the right to form a league for aggression and internal aggrandizement.

§ 60 [THE RIGHT OF A STATE AGAINST AN UNJUST ENEMY]

There is no limit to the rights of a state against an unjust enemy [*ungerechter Feind*] [3] (in respect to quantity or degree,

[3] [In this paragraph, I have translated *ungerecht* and *Ungerechtigkeit* by "unjust" and "injustice," respectively.]

although there are limits with respect to quality or kind). In other words, although an injured state may not use every means at its disposal in order to defend what belongs to it, it may use those means that are allowable in any amount or degree that it is able to do so. But what, then, is an *unjust enemy* according to concepts of the Law of nations, which holds that every state is a judge in its own cause as in a state of nature in general? An unjust enemy is someone whose publicly expressed Will (whether by words or by deeds) discloses a maxim that, if made into a universal rule, would make peace among nations impossible and would perpetuate the state of nature forever. An example of this would be the violation of public treaties, which, it can be assumed, is a matter that concerns every nation, inasmuch as their freedom is thereby threatened. And so all nations are called upon to unite against this mischief and to take away from the malefactor the power of committing it. But this does *not* include [the right of] causing a state at the same time to disappear from the face of the earth, so that its land will be distributed among the others. That would be an injustice against the people, who cannot lose their original right to unite into a commonwealth. They may be required, however, to adopt a new constitution that by its nature will be unfavorable to the passion for war.

As a matter of fact, the expression "an unjust enemy in a   350
state of nature" is a redundancy, for the state of nature is itself a condition of legal injustice. A just enemy would be one to whom I would do an injustice if I resisted him; but in that case he would also not be my enemy.

§ 61 [THE ESTABLISHMENT OF ENDURING PEACE]

Inasmuch as the state of nature among nations, just like that among individual men, is a condition that should be abandoned in favor of entering a lawful condition, all the rights of nations and all the external property of nations that can be acquired or preserved through war are merely provisional before this change takes place; only through the establishment of a universal union of states (in analogy to the union that makes a people into a state) can these rights become peremptory and a true state of peace be achieved. Because, however, such a state composed of nations would extend over vast regions, it would be too large to govern, and consequently the protection of each of its members would, in the end, be impossible, with the result that the multitude of such corporations would lead back to a state of war. It follows that perpetual peace (the ultimate goal of all of the Law of nations) is, of course, an Idea that cannot be realized. But the basic political principles that aim at this Idea by instructing us to enter such alliances of states as a means of continually approaching it closer are themselves feasible, inasmuch as continually attempting to approach this Idea is a requirement grounded in duty and in the rights of men and states.

Such a union of several states whose purpose is to preserve peace may be called the "permanent congress of states." Any neighboring state is free to join such a congress. We have an example of such a congress (at least as far as the [legal] formalities of the Law of nations relating to the preservation of peace are concerned) in the assembly of states-general at The Hague in the first half of this [the eighteenth] century. To this assembly, the ministers of most European courts and even of the smallest republics brought their complaints about the hostilities carried out by one against another. Thus, all of Europe thought of itself as a single federated state, which was supposed to fulfill the function of judicial arbitrator in these public disputes. Later, however, instead of this, the Law of nations disappeared from the cabinets [of these states] and survived only in books, or, after force had already been employed, it was relegated as a [useless] form of deduction to the darkness of the archives.

351 A congress, in the sense intended here, is merely a free and essentially arbitrary [willkürliche] combination of various states that can be dissolved at any time. As such, it should not be confused with a union (such as that of the American states) that is founded on a political constitution and which therefore cannot be dissolved. Only through the latter kind of

union can the Idea of the kind of public Law of nations that should be established become a reality, so that nations will settle their differences in a civilized way by judicial process, rather than in the barbaric way (of savages), namely, through war.

§ *third section* §
WORLD LAW
§ 62 [THE WORLD COMMUNITY]

The rational Idea of a peaceful, even if not friendly, universal community of all nations on earth that can come into mutual active relations with one another is not a philanthropic (ethical) principle, but a juridical one [*rechtliches Prinzip*]. From the fact that nature has enclosed all nations within a limited boundary (because of the spherical shape of the earth on which they live, as a *globus terraqueus*), it follows that any piece of land that is possessed by an inhabitant of the earth and on which he lives is only a part of a determinate whole, and, as such, everyone can be conceived as originally having a right to it.[1] Accordingly, all nations originally hold a community of the land, although it is not a juridical community of possession (*communio*), and therefore of use, or community of ownership of the same. The kind of community that they hold is that of possible physical interaction (*commercium*), that is, a community that involves a universal relationship of each to all the others such that they can offer to trade with one another; consequently, they have a right to attempt to trade with a foreigner without his being justified in regarding anyone who attempts it as an enemy. These rights and duties, insofar as they involve a possible unification of all nations for the purpose of establishing certain universal laws regarding their intercourse with one another, may be called *world Law (jus cosmopoliticum)* [*das weltbürgerliche Recht*].

1 [See §§ 13 ff.]

It might appear that oceans make a community of nations impossible. But this is not so, for, thanks to navigation, they provide the most favorable natural condition for commerce, which is even more lively when the coastlines are close to one another (as they are in the Mediterranean Sea). Nevertheless, frequent visits to strange coasts and, even more, the founding of colonies that are linked with a mother country provide an occasion for doing evil and violence to some place on our globe that will be felt everywhere. The fact that such abuse is possible does not nullify the right of a citizen of the earth to attempt [to establish] a community with everyone and to visit all the regions of the earth for this purpose. This right still does not, however, involve the right to colonize the land of another nation, for this requires a special contract.

At this point, the following question might be raised: Where lands have been newly discovered, may a nation settle and take possession of land in the neighborhood of a people who have already settled in that region, even without obtaining their consent?

If such a settlement takes place far enough away from the place where the first people live so that there will be no encroachment on their use of the land, then the right to do so is indubitable. If, however, the people are sheepherding or hunting tribes (like the Hottentots, the Tongas, or most of the American Indians) whose livelihood depends on large, wild tracts of land, such settlement should not be undertaken through violence, but only through a contract. Moreover, any such contract must not take advantage of the ignorance of the inhabitants in regard to the cession of their territory. Against this view, it might seem that there is ample justification for the use of violent means in this kind of situation because of the good for mankind that results from it. On the one hand, it is a means of bringing culture to primitive peoples (this is like the excuse that Büsching[2] offers for the bloody introduc-

2 [Anton Friedrich Büsching (1724–1793), German theologian and geographer. He wrote many works, principally on geography, of which the main one was the *Erdbeschreibung*, a description of the earth, in seven parts. He is often regarded as the founder of modern statistical geography.]

tion of Christianity into Germany), or, on the other hand, it is a means by which it is possible to clean out vagrants and criminals from one's own country, who, it is hoped, will improve themselves or their children in some other part of the world (like New Holland). Nevertheless, all these good intentions still cannot wash away the stains of injustice [*Ungerechtigkeit*] from the use of such means. Here, one might object that, had there been such scruples about using violence to start the erection of a lawful state of society, then perhaps the whole world would still be in a lawless condition. But such an argument will not succeed in invalidating the conditions of justice any more than does the excuse offered by revolutionaries, namely, that, when constitutions are evil, it is proper for the people to reform them by violent means and so generally to be unjust once and for all, in order thereafter to establish legal justice on a foundation that is so much more secure and to cause it to flourish.

CONCLUSION
[*Perpetual Peace*]

354

If one cannot prove that a certain thing exists, he can try to prove that it does not exist. If he succeeds in doing neither (as frequently happens), he can still ask whether he has any interest in accepting a conjecture that one or the other is true (hypothetically) and, if there is such an interest, whether it is a theoretical or a practical interest. Thus, from a theoretical point of view, we form a conjecture in order to explain a certain phenomenon (for example, for an astronomer, the phenomenon to be explained might be the retrograde motion of the planets). Or, on the other hand, from the practical point of view, we form a conjecture in order to attain some end; such an end may be either pragmatic (purely technological) or moral. If it is a moral end, it is one that duty requires us to adopt as a maxim. Now, it is evident that [although duty may require us to adopt an end as our maxim] it does not require us to conjecture (*suppositio*) the feasibility of the end in the sense in which such a conjecture is a purely theoretical judgment, and a problematic one as well, for there can be no obligation to do this (to believe something). What duty requires is that we act in accordance with the Idea of such an end, even if there is not the slightest theoretical probability that it is feasible, as long as its impossibility cannot be demonstrated either.

Now, moral-practical reason within us voices its irresistible veto: *There shall be no war,* either between thee and me in a state of nature or among states, which are still in a lawless condition in their external relations with one another, even though internally they are not. This is not the way in which anyone should prosecute his rights. Accordingly, there is no longer any question as to whether perpetual peace is a reality or a fiction and whether we deceive ourselves if we assume in a theoretical judgment that it is real. We must, however, act *as though* perpetual peace were a reality, which perhaps it is not, by working for its establishment and for the kind of constitution that seems best adapted for bringing it about (perhaps republicanism in every state). By this means [we may hope to] bring an end to the abominable practice of war, which up to now has been the chief purpose for which every state, without exception, has adapted its institutions. Even if the realization of this goal of abolishing war were always to remain just a pious wish, we still would certainly not be deceiving ourselves by adopting the maxim of working for it with unrelenting perseverance. Indeed, we have a duty to do so, and to assume that the moral law within us might deceive us would give rise to the disgusting wish to dispense with reason altogether and to conceive of ourselves and our principles as thrown in together with all the other species of animals under the same mechanism of nature.

As a matter of fact, it can be said that the establishment of a universal and enduring peace is not just a part, but rather constitutes the whole, of the ultimate purpose of Law [*Rechtslehre*] within the bounds of pure reason. When a number of men live together in the same vicinity, a state of peace is the only condition under which the security of property is guaranteed by laws, that is, when they live together under a constitution. Furthermore, the rule involved here is not a standard of conduct for others that is based on the experience of those who have hitherto found it most to their advantage. On the contrary, it must be derived a priori through reason from the Idea of a juridical association of men under public laws in general. In fact, every [empirical] example is deceptive (and can be used only to illustrate but not to prove [a principle]), and so a metaphysics is most certainly required. Even those who deride metaphysics still acknowledge its necessity when they say, for instance, as they often do: "The best constitution is one in which the power is exercised, not by men, but by the laws." What could be more sublimely metaphysical than this Idea? Yet it is an Idea that by their own admission possesses the most authentic objective reality, as can be easily shown in particular instances if need be. No attempt should be made, however, to realize this Idea precipitously through revolutionary methods, that is, by the violent overthrow of a previously existing imperfect and corrupt [government] (for in that case there would be an intervening moment when the entire juridical state of affairs would be annihilated). Instead, the Idea should be attempted and carried out through gradual reform according to fixed principles. Only in this way is it possible to approach continually closer to the highest political good—perpetual peace.

appendix

SUPPLEMENTARY EXPLANATIONS OF THE METAPHYSICAL ELEMENTS OF JUSTICE

The occasion for most of these remarks is provided by a review of this book that appeared in the *Göttingen Journal* (Number 28, February 18, 1797). In this review, the book is subjected to a penetrating and acute critical examination, but at the same time the reviewer writes with appreciative understanding and expresses "the hope that these *Elements* will remain a permanent contribution to knowledge." I shall use the remarks made in that review as a guide for my critical comments and for a further elaboration of the system.[1]

[On the Definition of the Faculty of Desire]

At the very beginning of the Introduction, my acute and critical reviewer finds a difficulty with a definition. What is meant by the faculty of desire? It is, according to the text, the capacity of being, by means of one's representations, the cause of the objects of those representations. In criticism of this definition, it is objected "that the definition amounts to nothing as soon as one abstracts from the external conditions of the consequences of desiring. But the faculty of desire is something that exists even for an idealist, although the external world does not exist for him."

1 [According to one of Fichte's letters, the reviewer was Prof. Friedrich Bouterwek of the University of Göttingen. A later publication by Bouterwek containing substantially the same criticisms bears this out. The complete review is reprinted in Kant's *Gesammelte Schriften* (Academie Ausgabe, Vol. XX, pp. 445–453, note).]

Answer: Are there not also intense yearnings that are consciously recognized to be in vain (for example, "Would to God that so and so were still alive!")? Indeed, such yearnings do not issue in overt action, nevertheless they are not entirely without consequences, namely, within the subject, although not in the external world. (They might, for example, make him ill.) Even when a subject perceives the inadequacy of his representations for producing the desired effect, it is still a mode of causality, at least internally within the subject.

The source of the misunderstanding is this: inasmuch as   357
(in the case under consideration) the consciousness of our capacity in general is at the same time also a consciousness of our incapacity with respect to the external world, the definition is not applicable for an idealist [because he denies the existence of the external world]. In the meantime, since only the relationship in general between the cause (the representation) and the effect (the feeling) is involved here [in this definition], the causality of the representation (whether it be external or internal causality) with respect to its object must inevitably be considered to be included in the concept of the faculty of desire.[2]

5. ADDITIONAL REMARKS IN ELUCIDATION OF   362
THE CONCEPT OF THE PENAL LAW

The mere Idea of a political constitution among men involves the concept of penal justice as an attribute of the supreme authority. The only question is whether the particular kind of punishment is a matter of indifference to the legislator as long as it serves as a means of suppressing crime (considered as a violation of the state's guarantee of the possession by each of what is his own) or whether the respect due the humanity in the person of the miscreant (that is, due the   363

[2] [Sections 1–4 and 6–7 are omitted, since they relate to sections under Part I that were also omitted. The headings are as follows:

1—Logical Propaedeutic to a Newly Ventured Concept of Right. 2—Justification of the Concept of a Personal Right That Is a Real Right. 3 —Examples. 4—Of the Confounding of Real and Personal Rights.]

human species) should also still be taken into account, simply on grounds of justice. I have contended that the *jus talionis* is the only principle of penal Law that accords with the form stipulated a priori by the Idea (which is not derived from experience, which could provide us with principles that would be the most effective means for achieving this purpose [that is, suppressing the crime]).[3] But how can this principle [of the equality of crime and punishment] be applied to punishments that do not allow reciprocation because they are either impossible in themselves or would themselves be punishable crimes against humanity in general? Rape, pederasty, and bestiality are examples of the latter. For rape and pederasty, [the punishment is] castration (after the manner of either a white or a black eunuch in the sultan's seraglio), and for bestiality the punishment] and when he suffers that which according to the criminal guilty of bestiality is unworthy of remaining in human society. *Per quod quis peccat, per idem punitur et idem.*[4]

These crimes are called unnatural because they are com-

[3] Every time a punishment is imposed, the sense of honor of the accused is (rightfully) hurt, because the imposition of punishment involves a purely one-sided use of coercion. As a result, the dignity of a citizen as such is, in this particular case, at least suspended, inasmuch as he is subjected to an external duty against which he, on his part, cannot bring any resistance. A man of noble rank or of wealth who has to pay a fine feels the humiliation of having to bow to the Will of a man of inferior status much more than the loss of the money. Penal justice (*justitia punitiva*), because it is based on arguments about punishability that are moral (*quia peccatum est*), must be sharply distinguished from that kind of punishment that is purely pragmatic and utilitarian (*ne peccetur*) and that is grounded on what experience has shown to be the most effective means of preventing crime. Penal justice has a quite different place (*locus justi*) in the topic * of concepts of justice and Law; it has neither the place of the *conducibilis* ["what is conducible to an end"] nor that of what is beneficial in some respect; indeed, it does not even occupy the place of the simple *honesti*, for the latter must be located under Ethics.

* [By "topic," Kant means, following Aristotle, "the places or sources from which arguments may be derived, or to which they may be referred"—*Webster's New International Dictionary* (2nd ed.), *s. v.*]

[4] ["He who commits a sin is punished through the same sin and in the same way."]

mitted against humanity itself [that is, against the purely human element in man]. To impose an arbitrary punishment for the same is contrary to the letter of penal justice. The only time a criminal cannot complain that he is treated unjustly is when he draws the evil deed back onto himself [as a punishment] and when he suffers that which according to the spirit of the penal law—even if not to the letter thereof—is the same as what he has inflicted on others.[5]

8. OF THE RIGHTS OF THE STATE RELATING TO PERPETUAL FOUNDATIONS FOR ITS SUBJECTS

367

An endowed foundation (*sanctio testamentaria beneficii perpetui*) is a voluntary institution sanctioned by the state and established for the benefit of a particular class of members of the state who follow one another successively until the whole class dies out. An endowed foundation is called "perpetual" when the enactment that establishes and maintains it is combined with the constitution of the state itself (inasmuch as the state must always be regarded as perpetual). These endowed foundations are, however, intended to benefit either the people in general or a part of the people united under a certain set of particular basic principles, a particular class, or a family and its descendants in perpetuity. Examples of the first kind of endowed foundation are hospitals; of the second, churches; of the third, orders (spiritual and secular); and, of the fourth, *majorats*.[6] Now, it is said that these corporations and their right of succession cannot be abolished because they have, through a testamentary will, become the property of the established heir, and to abrogate such a constitution [charter] would amount to taking a person's property from him.

[5] [Sections 6 and 7 are omitted. The headings are as follows: 6—Of the Right of Prescription. 7—Of Inheritance.]

[6] [A *majorat* is "an entailed estate, landed or funded, annexed to a title of honor and descending with it by primogeniture"—*Webster's New International Dictionary* (2nd ed.), *s. v.*]

A [Private Institutions for the Poor, Invalid, and Sick]

Those beneficent institutions for the poor, the invalid, and the sick that are financed from the state's funds (homes for the poor and hospitals) are certainly not subject to abolition. [But it is otherwise for private institutions, for,] if preference is to be given to the sense rather than to the letter of the Will of the testator [who has endowed them], in the course of time circumstances might arise that would make the abolition of such a foundation advisable, at least in its [present] form.

Thus, (with the exception of mental hospitals) it has been found that the poor and sick can be better and more cheaply cared for when a grant in aid of a certain sum of money (proportionate to the needs of the times) is made to the person concerned so that he can board wherever he pleases, with relatives or acquaintances; and this arrangement enables him to obtain better and cheaper care than he would have in a magnificent institution—such as the Greenwich Hospital—which is served by highly paid personnel, but where his freedom is nevertheless extremely limited. If such an arrangement is made as a substitute for foundations, it cannot be said that the state is taking away something that belongs to the people, namely, their enjoyment of the benefits of such foundations to which they have a justifiable claim; rather, it should be said that, in choosing wiser means for their support, the state is actually doing much more than before for their health and welfare.

B [The Church]

368

The clergy who do not propagate themselves by means of the body (that is, the Roman Catholic clergy) possess, with the approval of the state, landed estates and subjects attached to those lands, who belong to a spiritual state (called a church). The church is an institution to which lay people have given up themselves as pieces of deeded property in order to save their souls. Accordingly, as a special class of persons, the clergy has a [kind of] possession that can be legally transmitted from one age to the next, and this possession is sufficiently well attested in papal bulls. May we now assume that this [special] relationship of the clergy to the laity can be taken away from them through the absolute power of the secular state? If it is thus taken away, would it not mean that a person's property has been taken away from him by violence, just as was attempted by the unbelievers of the French Republic?

The question here is whether the church can belong to the state as its property or the state to the church as its property; for two supreme authorities cannot be subordinate to one another without implying a contradiction. It is perfectly clear that only the first [type of] constitution (*politico-hierarchica*) [that is, where the church belongs to the state] can be permanent, for every civil constitution is of this world, because it is an earthly authority (of men); and this fact, together with its consequences, can be documented by experience. The kingdom of the faithful is in the other world, in heaven, and, even if we grant them that there is a constitution relating to that other kingdom (*hierarchico-politica*), they still have to submit to the sufferings of the time under the supreme authority of men of this world. Hence, only the first [type of] constitution exists.

Religion (in the world of appearances) regarded as belief in the dogmas of the church and in the power of the priests, who are the aristocrats under such a [religious] constitution or even when the constitution is monarchical (papal)—religion in this sense can neither be imposed on the people nor taken away from them by any civil authority, nor, indeed, may the civil authority exclude a citizen from political services and the benefits that accompany them on the basis of a religious difference between the court and himself.

Now, in order to share in the grace that the church promises to procure for them even after death, certain devout and believing souls may establish an endowed foundation in perpetuity [with the intention that,] through such an act, certain landed estates are to become the property of the church after their death. In such circumstances, the state may pledge its allegiance and homage to the church in one respect or other or even to the church as a whole in order [to make it possible for its people to improve] their lot in the next world through prayers, indulgences, and penitences that the church's appointed ministers promise will be advantageous to them in the next world.[7] Nevertheless, even if such endowed foundations are supposedly established in perpetuity, their basis is by no means perpetual, since the state can, whenever it pleases, throw off the burden thus placed on it by the church.

The church is itself an institution founded merely on faith, and when, as a result of popular enlightenment, all the fraud and illusion disappear from these beliefs, the terrible authority of the clergy that is founded on them will fall away; and then the state will, with full right, seize the property that has been usurped by the church, that is, the land bequeathed to the church through testamentary wills. However, whenever this happens, the then-tenants of the previously existing institutions have the right to demand that they be indemnified for the rest of their lives.

If the specific character of any foundation for the poor or for education that is endowed in perpetuity is stipulated by the scheme [*Idee*] of its endowing founder, then such a foundation cannot [actually] be founded in perpetuity and so be a burden on the land. Rather, the state must have the freedom to adapt any endowed foundation to the needs of the time. On the other hand, no one should be surprised to find that it is not at all easy to carry out this Idea (for example, to require little paupers to beg by singing in order to make

7 [The German text is corrupt here. It is not only inconsistent grammatically, but some words are missing. Natorp suggests that the rest of the sentence after the brackets is misplaced and should be placed immediately after "believing souls." But his suggested change fails to account for the role and purpose of the state in its relation to the "devout souls" and the endowed foundations. If, as has been done here, a phrase like the one in brackets is inserted, the state's purpose in pledging allegiance, as well as permitting the endowed foundations, is explained. The present interpretation is entirely consistent with what Kant wrote earlier, in § 49 C, pp. 94–95.]

up for the inadequacy of those school funds that have been established by charity). Furthermore, a person who generously endows a foundation and at the same time is somewhat desirous of receiving glory therefrom does not want anyone with new ideas to alter his original plan, for he wants himself to be immortalized in the foundation. But none of this changes the nature of the things themselves and the right of the state, indeed its duty, to alter any foundation that is inconsistent with the state's preservation and its progress toward something better. Therefore, such a foundation can never be regarded as founded in perpetuity.

C [The Nobility]

The nobility in a country that is subject, not to an aristocratic, but to a monarchical constitution, is an institution that may well be allowed for a certain time, an institution that may even be made necessary by circumstances. Nevertheless, it is impossible to maintain that such a class could be founded in perpetuity and that the chief of state might not be authorized to abolish this class completely or that, were he to do so, he would be taking away from his (noble) subject something that was his. The nobility is a temporary confraternity authorized by the state; but it must adapt itself to the circumstances of the time and may not do violence to the universal rights of man, which have been suspended for so long.

370

The rank of nobleman in the state is not only dependent on the constitution itself, but is also merely an accidental [accretion] to the constitution, and as such it can exist in the state only in the mode of inherence. (A nobleman as such can be conceived of only in a civil state and not in the state of nature.) When, therefore, the state alters its constitution, no one who thereby loses his title and rank can claim that what is his has been taken away from him, inasmuch as his title and rank are his only under the condition that that particular form of the state remains the same, and the state [always] has the right to change its form (for example, to transform itself into a republic). Orders and the privilege of wearing certain insignia distinctive to these orders do not therefore establish any perpetual right of possession.

D [Majorats]

An endowed foundation that is called a *majorat* is established as follows: In appointing his heirs, a landowner stipulates that, in the series of successive heirs, always the nearest of kin to the family shall become the owner of the landed estate (by analogy to a monarchical political constitution where the lord of the country is determined in this way). Not only can such an endowment be abolished at any time with the consent of all agnates,[8] but it also may not endure in perpetuity, as though the right of inheritance were attached to the land. Instead, when such a federative system of the subjects of the state, who are like vice regents (analogous to dynasties or satrapies), has become extinct as the result of gradual reforms initiated by the state, the state has a right, indeed a duty, not to allow this system to be resuscitated.

CONCLUSION [*Duty to Obey the Powers That Be*]

Finally, the reviewer mentioned above makes the following observation in commenting on the Ideas presented under the heading of Public Law, with regard to which, as he says, there was no room left for further elaboration. He says:

371   To our knowledge, no philosopher has admitted the most paradoxical of all paradoxes, namely, the proposition that the mere Idea of sovereignty should necessitate me to obey as my lord anyone who has imposed himself upon me as a lord, without my asking who has given him the right to issue commands to me. Is there to be no difference between saying that one ought to recognize sovereignty and a chief of state and that one ought to hold a priori that this or that person, whose existence is not even given a priori, is one's lord?

Now, admitting that there is a paradox here, I hope that, when the view is examined more closely, it will at least not

8 [An "agnate" is a relative on the male side.]

be convicted of being heterodox. Furthermore, I hope that this judicious and conscientious reviewer, who has been so moderate in his criticisms (and who, despite the objection just mentioned, "regards these *Metaphysical Elements of Justice* on the whole as a contribution to knowledge"), will not be sorry for having taken my views under his protection against the spiteful and superficial condemnations of others and for having regarded my views as an attempt that is not unworthy of further examination.

The objectionable proposition in question is this: He who finds himself in possession of the supreme commanding and legislative authority over a people must be obeyed; and this [duty of obedience] is so unconditional juridically that it is in itself punishable to inquire publicly into the title of his acquisition [of this authority], that is, to raise questions about his title with a view to opposing him on the grounds of some defect in the title. In other words, a categorical imperative says: "Obey the suzerain (in everything that does not conflict with internal morality) who has authority over you!" But, not only is the reviewer perturbed by this principle, which makes a matter of fact (occupation or seizure) the condition that is the ground of a right, but he is even more shocked that the mere Idea of a sovereignty over a people should necessitate me, who belong to the people, to obey the usurped right without previously inquiring about it (§ 49 A [above]).

Every matter of fact is an object that is an appearance (of sense); on the other hand, that which can be represented only through pure reason and which must be included among the Ideas—that is the thing in itself. No object in experience can be given that adequately corresponds to an Idea. A perfect juridical [just] constitution among men would be an example of such an Idea.

When a people are united through laws under a suzerain, then the people are given as an object of experience conforming to the *Idea in general* of the unity of the people under a supreme powerful Will. Admittedly, this is only an appearance; that is, a juridical constitution in the most general sense   372 of the term is present. Although the [actual] constitution may contain grave defects and gross errors and may need to be gradually improved in important respects, still, as such, it is absolutely unpermitted and culpable to oppose it. If the people were to hold that they were justified in using violence against a constitution, however defective it might be, and against the supreme authority, they would be supposing that they had a right to put violence as the supreme prescriptive act of legislation in the place of every right and Law.

The Idea of a political constitution in general is holy and irresistible, [for] it is an Idea that is an absolute command of practical reason judging in accordance with concepts of justice—a command binding on every people. Even if the organization of the state is defective by itself, still no subordinate authority in that state can bring any active resistance against the legislative chief of that state. Rather, the deficiencies that are attributed to him must be gradually removed by reforms, which he carries out by himself. Otherwise, if a subject were to adopt a conflicting maxim (to proceed in accordance with his arbitrary will), a good constitution would come into being only as a result of blind chance.

The command, "Obey the suzerain who has authority over you," does not ruminate on how the suzerain acquired this authority (for the purpose, if need be, of undermining it). The authority that is now here and under which you live already possesses the [right of] legislation. Though you may indeed publicly discuss and debate this legislation, you cannot set yourselves up as opposing legislators.

The unconditional submission of the popular Will (which is in itself not united and hence is lawless) to the sovereign Will (uniting everyone through one single law) is a deed that can begin only with the seizure of the supreme authority and in this way provides a foundation for a public Law in the first place. To permit any opposition to this absolute power (an opposition that might limit that supreme authority) would be to contradict oneself, inasmuch as in that case the power (which may be opposed) would not be the lawful supreme authority that determines what is or is not to be publicly just. And this principle already resides a priori in the Idea of a political constitution in general, that is, in a concept of practical reason, a concept for which no adequately corresponding example from experience can be found, but one which, however, no one must contradict as a norm.

GLOSSARY

Anfangsgrund *	element	Gesetzwidrig	unlawful
		Gewalt (1)	authority
Befehlshaber	magistrate	Gewalt (2)	violence
Befugnis	authorization,	Grundsatz	basic principle
	liberty, com-		
	petence	Habe	belongings,
Befugt	authorized		possessions
Beherrscher	sovereign	Herrscher	sovereign
Bemächtigung	occupation		
Besitz	possession	Idee *	Idea
Besitznehmen	take possession	Inhabung *	detention
Bürgerliche			
Gesellschaft	civil society	Landesherr	master or lord
			of the country
Dingliches		Macht	power
Recht	right *in rem*	Meine, das *	what is mine,
Deine, das	what is yours,		my property
	your property	Meine, das, und	
	(*see* Meine)	das Deine *	property
Eigentum	what is owned	Oberbefehls-	chief com-
	(*dominium*)	haber	mander,
Eigentümer	owner (*domi-*		supreme
	nus)		commander
Ethik	Ethics	Obere, Ober-	
		haupt, Oberst	suzerain
Gemein Wesen	commonwealth	Obrigkeit	suzerainty
Gerecht	just		
Gerechtigkeit *	legal justice	Pflicht	duty
Gesetz *	law		
Gesetzlich	lawful	Recht *	justice, Law,
Gesetzlos	lawless		right
Gesetzmässig	legal	Recht, mit	rightfully
Gesetzmässig-		Rechtsbegriff	concept of jus-
keit	legality		tice

* Words marked with an asterisk are discussed in the Translator's
Introduction.

Rechtens	Lawful, according to the Law of the land	Tugendlehre *	ethics
Rechtsgelehrte	jurist	Unrecht tun	do an injustice (to someone)
Rechtskräftig	having the force of law	Unrechtmässig	illegitimate
Rechtslehre *	jurisprudence, justice, Law	Unrechtmässig- keit	illegitimacy
		Ungesetzmässig	illegal
Rechtlich	juridical, right- ful, de jure	Ungesetzmässig- keit	illegality
Rechtmässig	legitimate	Ursprünglicher Vertrag	original con- tract
Rechtmässigkeit	legitimacy		
Rechtswidrig	contrary to law		
Regent,		Verbinden	bind, obligate
Regierer	ruler	Verbindlichkeit	obligation
Regierung	the government	Verpflichten	to bind to a duty
		Verpflichtungs- sart *	way of being bound to a duty
Seine, das	one's own, one's property (see Meine)		
Sittenlehre	moral philoso- phy, theory of morals	Wille *	Will
		Willkür *	will
Staatsoberhaupt	chief of state	Zurechnung	imputation
Strafrecht	penal law, penal justice	Zustand	condition, state of affairs, state
Triebfeder	incentive	Zwang	coercion

* Words marked with an asterisk are discussed in the Translator's Introduction.

INDEX

The Library of Liberal Arts

Below is a representative selection from The Library of Liberal Arts. This partial listing—taken from the more than 200 scholarly editions of the world's finest literature and philosophy—indicates the scope, nature, and concept of this distinguished series.

THE AMERICAN HERITAGE SERIES

THE COLONIAL PERIOD

THE REVOLUTIONARY ERA

THE YOUNG NATION

TOPICAL VOLUMES